في ذكرى

مارك لينز

Karl-Josef Kuschel is Professor Emeritus of Catholic Theology at the University of Tübingen, Germany. He taught the theology of culture and inter-religious dialogue and was the deputy director of Institute of Ecumenical and Inter-Religious Studies. He was a member of the advisory board of Theology and Literature (London). From 1995 to 2009 he was vice president of the Stiftung Weltethos, working closely with his doctoral supervisor and founding president of Weltethos Hans Küng.

KARL-JOSEF KUSCHEL

Christmas and the Qur'an

Translated by Simon Pare

GINGKO

First published in the United Kingdom in 2017 by
Gingko
4 Molasses Row, London SW11 3UX

This first paperback edition published in 2020

First published in German as *Weihnachten und der Koran* by Karl-Josef Kuschel

Cover illustration: Chester Beatty Library Per 231.227, Maryam (Mary) Shakes a Palm Tree to Provide Food for the Baby Isa (Jesus) © The Trustees of the Chester Beatty Library, Dublin

A CIP catalogue record for the book is available from the British Library

ISBN 978-1-909942-38-7
eISBN 978-1-909942-06-6

Typeset in Optima by MacGuru Ltd

Printed in the UK

www.gingko.org.uk
@gingkolibrary

Contents

Christians and Muslims should go beyond tolerance, accepting differences, while remaining aware of commonalities and thanking God for them. They are called to mutual respect, thereby condemning derision of religious beliefs.

Generalisation should be avoided when speaking of religions. Differences of confessions within Christianity and Islam, diversity of historical contexts are important factors to be considered.

Religious traditions cannot be judged on the basis of a single verse or a passage present in their respective holy Books. A holistic vision as well as an adequate hermeneutical method is necessary for a fair understanding of them.

Joint declaration of the Pontifical Council for Inter-religious Dialogue (Vatican) and the Centre for Inter-religious Dialogue of the Islamic Culture and Relations Organisation (Tehran) held in Rome, 28–30 April 2008.[1]

Foreword to the English edition

This book was written in a spirit of dialogue. The author is a Christian theologian who has spent many years trying to acquire a better understanding of Islam, mainly by studying the Qur'an in depth and comparing it to the Bible to prepare the ground for dialogue between Christians and Muslims. This book is the fruit of my detailed consideration of how the Bible and the Qur'an relate to each other, and it is underpinned by my conviction that our Holy Scriptures contain within themselves the foundations for a discussion of core articles of faith.

Dialogue does not mean equivalence, nor does it mean denying or playing down the fact that there are enduring differences between Christian and Muslim beliefs. However, in a positive sense, dialogue means doing everything we can to understand each other better, by studying the relevant texts and meeting people. And understanding each other better means analysing, as far as is appropriate, what we have in common and what divides us so that we may learn to respect each other's otherness. The Qur'an does not incite Jews, Christians and Muslims to nurture contempt or even hostility towards each other, but rather to 'be foremost in good works' (Sura 5:48).[2] In writing this book I have taken those words very seriously.

As a result of my long studies and many encounters with Muslims I too have come to the conclusion that Christians and Muslims 'should go beyond tolerance, accepting differences, while remaining aware of commonalities and thanking God for them,' to quote from a joint declaration of the Pontifical Council for Inter-religious Dialogue (Vatican) and the Centre for Inter-religious Dialogue of the Islamic Culture and Relations Organisation (Tehran) in 2008.

My advocacy for serious dialogue between Christians and Muslims goes back a good twenty-five years to my discovery of the 'Abrahamic' root from which Judaism, Christianity and Islam are sprung. All three religions revere Abraham as the father of their faith, from whom they learned the central lesson for humankind before God – proven trust. The Hebrew Bible describes Abraham as a blessing for 'all the families of the earth' (Gen 12:2–3); in the New Testament, Abraham is 'the father of us all […] in the presence of Him whom he believed – God' (Romans 4:16–17); according to the Qur'an, Abraham is a 'leader of people' (Sura 2:124). However, Jews, Christians and Muslims do not believe 'in Abraham' but in the god to whom he pays tribute as the creator, protector and judge of humankind. Hence, all three Holy Books call Abraham the 'friend of God': the prophet Isaiah (Isa. 41:8), the New Testament Book of James (James 2:23) and Sura 4:125 in the Qur'an.

My discovery of this Abrahamic root had significant

consequences for my subsequent work, and I explored it in my two previous books. The first was *Abraham: Sign of Hope for Jews, Christians and Muslims*[3] and the second is titled *Die Bibel im Koran. Grundlagen für das interreligiöse Gespräch (The Bible in the Qur'an. Foundations for Interreligious Dialogue, 2017).*[4] I think that the Holy Scriptures themselves provide an opportunity for Jews, Christians and Muslims no longer to ostracise one another as 'infidels', 'unredeemed', 'out-dated' or 'deficient' (as has so often been the case throughout history), but instead to show mutual regard for one another as 'children of Abraham', all pursuing their own paths before God and towards God. Jews, Christians and Muslims share a common heritage that sets them apart from other religions – for instance, Asian religions such as Hinduism, Buddhism and Confucianism. This includes the stories of Adam and the Creation, Noah and his rescue from the Great Flood, Moses and his struggle against a heathen despot, Joseph and his tumultuous fate under God's wing, and David, to whom God gave his own book, the Psalms (to name but a few examples). This is not a value judgment: it merely illustrates that Jews, Christians and Muslims have a duty to acknowledge their shared responsibility before God as 'children of Abraham' for the common good of humankind.

Reading the Bible and the Qur'an alongside each other is an important act of faith in an age of division like ours, when 'religion' is often misused in order to divide people and stoke distrust and hatred. Other studies have laid the groundwork. I can think of a group of French Christian and Muslim researchers, whose first publication, in 1987, was *Ces Écritures qui nous questionnent: La Bible et le Coran (The Challenge of the Scriptures. The Bible and the Qur'an*, New York 1989). I can also think of major studies by the Canadian Christian theologian Brian Arthur Brown, including *Noah's Other Son. Bridging the Gap between the Bible and the Qur'an* (New York/London 2007) and *Three Testaments. Torah, Gospel and Quran* (New York/Toronto/Plymouth UK 2012). I'm also thinking of an exciting undertaking by the British Christian scholar of Islam Colin Chapman called *The Bible Through Muslim Eyes and a Christian Response* (Cambridge 2008), which was written in the hope that 'one day, a Muslim in Great Britain will write a book with a similar title, "The Qur'an Through Christian Eyes and a Muslim Response"'. There is also a book published in response to the pioneering, even sensational, *A Common Word*, a text signed by 138 Muslim scholars in 2007. It's called *A Common Word: Muslims and Christians on Loving God and Neighbor* by Miroslav Volf, Ghazi bin Muhammad and Melissa Yarrington (Grand Rapids, MI/Cambridge UK 2010), but more on that in the sixth and final chapter of this book. I should also mention the subsequent project by the US Christian theologian Barbara J. Hampton, *Reading Scripture Together. A Comparative Qur'an and Bible Study Guide* (2014). Last but not least, there are also many small initiatives in German cities. Erlangen deserves a special mention, for young people there have organised a 'Café Abraham', creating a forum for Jews, Christians and Muslims to meet, help each other and talk.

Another thing that is especially important for Christians is that they also share with Muslims the story of **John**, whom the Qur'an calls a prophet (Sura 3:39) and the New Testament, the 'Baptist' (Matt. 3:1–8), **Jesus**, who is venerated among Muslims as 'a messenger' (Sura 5:75) and by Christians as the 'Son of God' (Luke 1:32), and **Mary**, who is a particularly blessed woman for Christians and Muslims alike (Luke 1:30) and 'chosen' by God (Sura 3:42). Mary, the mother of Jesus, is the only woman mentioned by name in the Qur'an, which explains the high regard in which devout Muslims hold Mary to this day. This book will discuss these matters in detail. Such 'overlaps' between the two traditions bind Christians and Muslims together in a special religious community, even though the Qur'an explicitly does not acknowledge an entirely new revelation, unprecedented in religious history, which expunges all prior revelations. Rather, the Qur'an seeks to restore the ancient religion that God had previously entrusted to Jews and Christians: the 'religion of Abraham' (Sura 2:130–135). The Qur'an therefore appeals to Muslims:

Say, 'We believe in God and in what was sent down
to us

and in what was sent down to Abraham, Isaac,
   Ishmael, Jacob and the tribes,
and in what was given to Moses and Jesus
and all the prophets by their Lord.
We make no distinction between any of them,
and we devote ourselves to Him.' (Sura 2:136)

What is of particular significance to Christians is that the Qur'an attaches great importance – indeed, a profound theological interpretation – to the **birth of Jesus**. Both Sura 19:16–35 and Sura 3:45–59 report God's annunciation to Mary, the birth of her son and his deeds in such a manner that Jesus becomes a 'sign to all people' and a sign of God's 'blessing' (Sura 19:21). Furthermore, Sura 19:32 explicitly states that Jesus is 'not domineering' but a man of 'peace'. 'Peace was on me,' the Qur'an quotes Jesus as saying, 'the day I was born and will be on the day I die, and the day I am raised to life again' (Sura 19:33).

The birth of Jesus is also recounted in two books in the Christian Bible: the Gospel According to Matthew and Luke's Gospel. I have tried to establish a conversation between these two traditions – the Qur'an and the New Testament – in my book. In doing so, I have analysed both the differences and the similarities between them, and demonstrated that the story of the birth of Jesus is more suitable than virtually any other for comparing the Holy Scriptures and prompting exchanges across religious boundaries to bring Christians and Muslims together in a spirit of dialogue. My book will provide some answers as to why this is the case.

All too often in the past, communities have lived alongside each other in mutual indifference. There has been too much ignorance on all sides, often combined with arrogance regarding one's own religion's supposed superiority over all others. It is high time, however, to make the early years of the third millennium a period of exchange between religions, the beginning of a new culture of inter-religious communication. There are too few peaceful initiatives, rather than too many, in our turbulent world, which is regularly shaken by acts of violence. How it would build confidence between believers around the world if Christians and Muslims were to take the message of peace seriously! The feast of Christmas is the ideal occasion for this, as Christians and Muslims could exchange wishes of peace: 'Peace be with you and yours and on your house and family.' This would foster trust and peaceful coexistence in neighbourhoods, towns and communities where Christians and Muslims live together. It would encourage a culture of attentiveness to the presence of others as an alternative to the barbarism of mistrust and exclusion. Peace could reign in the name of Him who was announced to Mary in the following words: 'Mary, God gives you news of a Word from Him, whose name will be the Messiah, Jesus, son of Mary, who will be held in honour in this world and the next, who will be one of those brought near to God' (Sura 3:45). Christianity and

Islam influence the behaviour of over two billion people on this planet. If they cannot come to terms, then the world as a whole will never live in peace.

I am extremely happy to be able to share my thoughts with English-speaking readers in Simon Pare's translation, which joins Italian and Persian editions of the book. I would like to thank him for his patient, painstaking and committed work. I hope that this book will encourage people to strive even harder to promote dialogue.

Tübingen, August 2017
Karl-Josef Kuschel

Christians and Muslims Meet at Christmas

I can recall the precise moment that triggered this book. In the late 1980s I was invited to Ahlen in Westphalia to share the subject of my book *Abraham: Sign of Hope for Jews, Christians and Muslims* (1995) with a wider audience. No sooner had I arrived than I was whisked off on a memorial trail through the old town, which was designed to remind people of the fate of the town's Jews after 1933. A community group had decided quite literally to embed these memories in the cobbles of their hometown as a memorial and a warning to future generations. One hundred names of Holocaust victims from Ahlen are engraved on an impressive monument, which was inaugurated in 1985 on the site of the former Jewish community centre in Klosterstrasse. A book devoted to the history of Ahlen's Jews bears the title *Der Weg nach Auschwitz began auch in Ahlen* (*The Road to Auschwitz Began in Ahlen Too* – untranslated) (1988).

I was also told about a special Christian-Muslim project in Ahlen and given a newspaper cutting about an event that had taken place on 24 December 1986:

The Catholic parish of St Joseph in Ahlen in
Westphalia wishes to take greater steps to entertain
good neighbourly relations with the congregation of
the town's Turkish Muslim mosque. A parish councillor
explained to Deutsche Welle radio that an event last
Christmas Eve was the catalyst for this decision. Two
representatives of the nearby mosque appeared at
the church with a ceremonial bouquet during Mass
to present to the congregation the greetings and
good wishes of all Muslim residents of Ahlen on the
feast of the birth of Jesus. This 'sign of affection and
generosity' met with 'spontaneous applause' from the
congregation. At the same time, many Christians felt
ashamed that they had barely acknowledged any of
the major Islamic feasts up to that point. The events
of that Christmas Eve raised people's hopes of good
cooperation 'with our Muslim brothers and sisters':
'This meeting was in the true spirit of Christmas, and
it will change our hitherto indifferent attitude towards
our Muslim neighbours into one of sincere regard and
empathy.'[5]

That scene stuck in my mind. I kept the newspaper cutting
in a safe place and have referred to it many times since in
my lectures. This scene reveals a surprising spirit, doesn't
it? For let us not fool ourselves: our society has greatly
degraded, degenerated and devalued 'Christmas' into
a festival largely devoid of religious meaning, spiritual

substance and ethical commitment. In Germany too, we have allowed this great religious feast to decline to a point where it is on the verge of disappearance. A century ago the author Hermann Hesse expressed an opinion that is still valid today: 'Our Christmas has long been a senti-mental occasion, with the exception of a few truly devout people. In part it has become something even worse: an excuse for advertising, an opportunity for attempted scams, and fertile ground for the production of kitsch.'

Through a dialogue with Muslims, however, the message of Christmas *could* be re-energised, as Muslims also cele-brate the birth of Jesus as a 'sign from God' to humankind. Together, Christians and Muslims could commemorate this fact, thereby *potentially* becoming the trustees and guardi-ans of the theocentric message of Christmas, in defiance of all the degradation, kitsch and sentimentality. So I pricked up my ears when 138 Muslim scholars from around the world wished Christians a peaceful Christmas in 2007, something without historical precedent. The Christmas message was published by the Royal Aal-al-Bayt Institute for Islamic Thought in Amman in Jordan, and drawn up by a group including representatives of both major Muslim denominations, Sunnis and Shias, as well as followers of Sufism. The message ran as follows:

In the Name of God, the Compassionate, the Merciful
May God bless Muhammad and his kin and bless
* Abraham and his kin*

Al-Salaamu Aleikum; Peace be upon you; pax vobiscum

Peace be upon Jesus Christ who says, 'Peace is upon me the day I was born, the day I die, and the day I am resurrected' (Chapter of Mary; the Holy Qur'an; 19:34).

During these joyful holidays we write to you, our Christian neighbours all over the world, to express our thanks for the beautiful and gracious responses that we Muslims have been receiving from the very first day we issued our invitation to come together to 'A Common Word' based on 'Love of God and Love of Neighbour'.[6]

We thank you and wish you all a joyous and peaceful Christmas Holiday Season commemorating the birth of Jesus Christ, may peace be upon him.

We Muslims bear witness that: *There is no god but God, without associate, and that Muhammad is His Servant and Messenger, and that Jesus is His Servant, His Messenger, His Word cast to Mary, and a Spirit from Him…. (Sahih Bukhari, Kitab Ahadith al-Anbiya').*

We pray, during these blessed days, which have coincided with the Muslim feast of the *Hajj* or Pilgrimage, which commemorates the faith of the Prophet Abraham (peace be upon him), that the New Year may bring healing and peace to our suffering world. God's refusal to let Abraham (peace be upon him) sacrifice his son – granting him instead a ram

– is to this day a Divine warrant and a most powerful social lesson for all the followers of the Abrahamic faiths, to ever do their utmost to save, uphold and treasure every single human life and especially the life of every single child. Indeed, it is worthy of note that this year Muslim scholars issued a historic declaration affirming the sanctity of human life – *of every human life* – as an essential and foundational teaching in Islam upon which all Muslim scholars are in unanimous agreement.[7]

May the coming year be one in which the sanctity and dignity of human life is upheld by all. May it be a year of humble repentance before God, and mutual forgiveness within and between communities.

Praise be to God, the Lord of the worlds.

Thank you for the 'beautiful and gracious responses'? A 'historic declaration'? This refers to the fact that this same group of 138 Muslim clerics had published a letter to Pope Benedict XVI and many Christian leaders in mid-October 2007, calling, in what counts as a dramatic appeal, for a dialogue between Christians and Muslims. I mentioned it already in my foreword. For 'the first time since the days of the Prophet', it says, Islamic clerics have come together as one to declare 'the commonalities between Islam and Christianity'. What are these 'commonalities'? The Two Commandments of Love! Long passages of the document proceed to justify these two commandments to love God and to love one's neighbour with reference to the Qur'an and the Sunna (the transmitted record of the teachings, acts and sayings of the Prophet). The text also draws attention to parallels with the Old and New Testaments, concluding: 'Thus the Unity of God, love of Him, and love of the neighbour form a common ground upon which Islam and Christianity (and Judaism) are founded.' We shall return to this document in Chapter 6, where it will be critically discussed.

Muslims wishing Christians 'a joyous and peaceful Christmas Holiday Season commemorating the birth of Jesus Christ'? How are we to assess this declaration? As a polite gesture, a diplomatic manoeuvre, a purely political step in a precarious global climate? All of those, certainly. But Muslims' own Holy Scripture offers them plenty of compelling reasons for commemorating the birth of Jesus in special fashion.[8] For the Qur'an presents the 'Christmas story' – the story of Jesus' birth – in great detail. As does the New Testament, it discusses the Annunciation to Mary, Jesus' conception by the Holy Spirit, and the virgin birth. Reasons enough to take a closer look and to set myself a challenge – Christmas and the Qur'an! A call for a fuller dialogue between Christians and Muslims about the fundamental tenets of their faiths. That is the dialogue this book hopes to instigate, and I shall do so through precise examination of the primary sources: the New Testament and the Qur'an.

PART ONE

The Birth of Jesus in the New Testament

Our story is subliminally infused with the tension between the universal claims of the Roman ruler, who had based the *Pax Romana,* as a *Pax Augustana,* on the strength of the Roman legions, and the universal claims of the Jewish [...] Messiah, who was crucified by a Roman prefect, Pontius Pilate, after proclaiming God's dominion and preaching non-violence.

Rudolf Pesch, *Das Weihnachtsevangelium*
(*The Christmas Gospel,* 2007)

If, instead of the Three Kings, Confucius, Lao-tzu and Buddha had travelled from the Orient to the crib, only one of them – Lao-tzu – would have recognised, though not worshipped, the insignificance of the Almighty. But even he would not have recognised the stumbling block that Christian love represented in a world of established connections and stratified hierarchies based on domination. Jesus is the countersign to this domination, and it is precisely this sign that is countered through the gallows.

Ernst Bloch, *The Principle of Hope* (1969)

The 'Christmas story' has been called the 'best-known story in world literature'[9] and that is probably no exaggeration. Its influence on religion – not to mention culture, literature, music and painting – is immeasurable. Yet Jesus' birth is obscured by the veil of history. The New Testament accounts have too obviously been composed according to a model of predestination to be accepted as *historical* sources. Prophecies made in the Hebrew Bible are fulfilled and confirmed by frequent quotes from the books of the Prophets. Everything is so bathed in the light of extraordinary events – angelic apparitions, the Immaculate Conception by the Holy Spirit, cosmic events directing 'astrologers', the new-born baby's rescue from murderous attacks – that it is impossible to separate fact from fiction. We also find variations on these miraculous signs accompanying the birth of the founders of other religions, for example Moses and Buddha, but also Muhammad, as we shall see and investigate in a separate chapter devoted to the accounts of Muhammad's birth.

1. The primary sources

What is striking, however, is that the Christian primary sources are relatively restrained in contrast to the wealth of detail provided by later texts known as the Infancy Gospels.[10] Moreover, the majority of the New Testament is completely uninterested in stories of Jesus' birth. The Evangelists Mark and John provide no birth accounts whatsoever and nor does St Paul: there is not a single word about the Bethlehem tradition in any of Paul's epistles.

Only Matthew's and Luke's Gospels relate the story of Jesus' birth, but they do so in a way that reveals not its mythical and eternal features, but rather the immediate, temporal aspects of events. The New Testament stories testify to the fact that the accounts are still in flux when it comes to the birth of the 'Messiah'. Many of their characteristics are not yet definite, and many details still vary. The broad mythical and legendary traits are not fully fleshed out, as is usual with 'founding fathers'. The very fact that there are two very different accounts merely serves to underline this. So let us first take a few minutes to examine these two texts.[11]

God's peace on Earth: the story according to Luke

1

Inasmuch as many have taken in hand to set in order a narrative of those things which have been fulfilled among us, just as those who from the beginning were eyewitnesses and ministers of the word delivered them to us, it seemed good to me also, having had perfect understanding of all things from the very first, to write to you an orderly account, most excellent Theophilus, that you may know the certainty of those things in which you were instructed.

There was in the days of Herod, the king of Judea, a certain priest named Zachariah, of the division of Abijah. His wife was of the daughters of Aaron, and her name was Elizabeth. And they were both righteous before God, walking in all the commandments and ordinances of the Lord blameless. But they had no child, because Elizabeth was barren, and they were both well advanced in years.

So it was, that while he was serving as priest before God in the order of his division, according to the custom of the priesthood, his lot fell to burn incense when he went into the temple of the Lord. And the whole multitude of the people was praying outside at the hour of incense. Then an angel of the Lord appeared to him, standing on the right side of the altar of incense. And when Zachariah saw him, he was troubled, and fear fell upon him.

But the angel said to him, 'Do not be afraid, Zachariah, for your prayer is heard; and your wife Elizabeth will bear you a son, and you shall call his name John. And you will have joy and gladness, and many will rejoice at his birth. For he will be great in the sight of the Lord, and shall drink neither wine nor strong drink. He will also be filled with the Holy Spirit, even from his mother's womb. And he will turn many of the children of Israel to the Lord their God. He will also go before Him in the spirit and power of Elijah, to turn the hearts of the fathers to the children, and the disobedient to the wisdom of the just, to make ready a people prepared for the Lord.'

And Zachariah said to the angel, 'How shall I know this? For I am an old man, and my wife is well advanced in years.'

And the angel answered and said to him, 'I am Gabriel, who stands in the presence of God, and was sent to speak to you and bring you these glad tidings. But behold, you will be mute and not able to speak until the day these things take place, because you did not believe my words which will be fulfilled in their own time.'

And the people waited for Zachariah, and marvelled that he lingered so long in the temple. But when he came out, he could not speak to them; and they perceived that he had seen a vision in the temple, for he beckoned to them and remained speechless.

So it was, as soon as the days of his service were completed, that he departed to his own house. Now after those days his wife Elizabeth conceived; and she hid herself five months, saying, 'Thus the Lord has dealt with me, in the days when He looked on me, to take away my reproach among people.'

Now in the sixth month the angel Gabriel was sent by God to a city of Galilee named Nazareth, to a virgin betrothed to a man whose name was Joseph, of the house of David. The virgin's name was Mary. And having come in, the angel said to her, 'Rejoice, highly favoured one, the Lord is with you; blessed are you among women!'

But when she saw him, she was troubled at his saying, and considered what manner of greeting this was. Then the angel said to her, 'Do not be afraid, Mary, for you have found favour with God. And behold, you will conceive in your womb and bring forth a Son, and shall call His name Jesus. He will be great, and will be called the Son of the Highest; and the Lord God will give Him the throne of His father David. And He will reign over the house of Jacob forever, and of His kingdom there will be no end.'

Then Mary said to the angel, 'How can this be, since I do not know a man?'

And the angel answered and said to her, 'The Holy Spirit will come upon you, and the power of the Highest will overshadow you; therefore, also, that Holy One who is to be born will be called the Son of God. Now indeed, Elizabeth your relative has also conceived a son in her old age; and this is now the sixth month for her who was called barren. For with God nothing will be impossible.'

Then Mary said, 'Behold the maidservant of the Lord! Let it be to me according to your word.' And the angel departed from her.

Now Mary arose in those days and went into the hill country with haste, to a city of Judah, and entered the house of Zachariah and greeted Elizabeth. And it happened, when Elizabeth heard the greeting of Mary, that the babe leaped in her womb; and Elizabeth was filled with the Holy Spirit. Then she spoke out with a loud voice and said, 'Blessed are you among women, and blessed is the fruit of your womb! But why is this granted to me, that the mother of my Lord should come to me? For indeed, as soon as the voice of your greeting sounded in my ears, the babe leaped in my womb for joy. Blessed is she who believed, for there will be a fulfilment of those things which were told her from the Lord.'

And Mary said:

'My soul magnifies the Lord,

And my spirit has rejoiced in God my Saviour.

For He has regarded the lowly state of His
    maidservant;

For behold, henceforth all generations will call me
    blessed.

For He who is mighty has done great things for me,

And holy is His name.

And His mercy is on those who fear Him

From generation to generation.

He has shown strength with His arm;

He has scattered the proud in the imagination of
    their hearts.

He has put down the mighty from their thrones,

And exalted the lowly.

He has filled the hungry with good things,

And the rich He has sent away empty.

He has helped His servant Israel,

In remembrance of His mercy,

As He spoke to our fathers,

To Abraham and to his seed forever.'

And Mary remained with her about three months, and returned to her house.

Now Elizabeth's full time came for her to be delivered, and she brought forth a son. When her neighbours and relatives heard how the Lord had shown great mercy to her, they rejoiced with her.

So it was, on the eighth day, that they came to circumcise the child; and they would have called him by the name of his father, Zachariah. His mother answered and said, 'No; he shall be called John.'

But they said to her, 'There is no one among your relatives who is called by this name.' So they made signs to his father – what he would have him called.

And he asked for a writing tablet, and wrote, saying, 'His name is John.' So they all marvelled. Immediately his mouth was opened and his tongue loosed, and he spoke, praising God. Then fear came on all who dwelt around them; and all these sayings were discussed throughout all the hill country of Judea. And all those who heard them kept them in their hearts, saying, 'What kind of child will this be?' And the hand of the Lord was with him.

Now his father Zachariah was filled with the Holy

Spirit, and prophesied, saying:
    'Blessed is the Lord God of Israel,
    For He has visited and redeemed His people,
    And has raised up a horn of salvation for us
    In the house of His servant David,
    As He spoke by the mouth of His holy prophets,
    Who have been since the world began,
    That we should be saved from our enemies
    And from the hand of all who hate us,
    To perform the mercy promised to our fathers
    And to remember His holy covenant,
    The oath which He swore to our father Abraham:
    To grant us that we,
    Being delivered from the hand of our enemies,
    Might serve Him without fear,
    In holiness and righteousness before Him all the
        days of our life.
    And you, child, will be called the prophet of the
        Highest;
    For you will go before the face of the Lord to
        prepare His ways,
    To give knowledge of salvation to His people
    By the remission of their sins,
    Through the tender mercy of our God,
    With which the Dayspring from on high has visited
        us;
    To give light to those who sit in darkness and the
        shadow of death,

To guide our feet into the way of peace.'

So the child grew and became strong in spirit, and was in the deserts till the day of his manifestation to Israel.

II

And it came to pass in those days that a decree went out from Caesar Augustus that all the world should be registered. This census first took place while Quirinius was governing Syria. So all went to be registered, everyone to his own city.

Joseph also went up from Galilee, out of the city of Nazareth, into Judea, to the city of David, which is called Bethlehem, because he was of the house and lineage of David, to be registered with Mary, his betrothed wife, who was with child. So it was, that while they were there, the days were completed for her to be delivered. And she brought forth her firstborn Son, and wrapped Him in swaddling cloths, and laid Him in a manger, because there was no room for them in the inn.

Now there were in the same country shepherds living out in the fields, keeping watch over their flock by night. And behold, an angel of the Lord stood before them, and the glory of the Lord shone around them, and they were greatly afraid. Then the angel said to them, 'Do not be afraid, for behold, I bring you good tidings of great joy which will be to all people. For there is born to you this day in the city of David a Saviour, who is Christ the Lord. And this will be the sign to you: You will find a Babe wrapped in swaddling cloths, lying in a manger.'

And suddenly there was with the angel a multitude of the heavenly host praising God and saying:

'Glory to God in the highest,

And on earth peace, goodwill toward men!'

So it was, when the angels had gone away from them into heaven, that the shepherds said to one another, 'Let us now go to Bethlehem and see this thing that has come to pass, which the Lord has made known to us.' And they came with haste and found Mary and Joseph, and the Babe lying in a manger. Now when they had seen Him, they made widely known the saying which was told them concerning this Child. And all those who heard it marvelled at those things which were told them by the shepherds. But Mary kept all these things and pondered them in her heart. Then the shepherds returned, glorifying and praising God for all the things that they had heard and seen, as it was told them.

(Luke 1:1 – 2:20)

A child of the Holy Spirit: the story according to Matthew

I

So all the generations from Abraham to David are

fourteen generations, from David until the captivity in Babylon are fourteen generations, and from the captivity in Babylon until the Christ are fourteen generations.

Now the birth of Jesus Christ was as follows: After His mother Mary was betrothed to Joseph, before they came together, she was found with child of the Holy Spirit. Then Joseph her husband, being a just man, and not wanting to make her a public example, was minded to put her away secretly. But while he thought about these things, behold, an angel of the Lord appeared to him in a dream, saying, 'Joseph, son of David, do not be afraid to take to you Mary your wife, for that which is conceived in her is of the Holy Spirit. And she will bring forth a Son, and you shall call His name Jesus, for He will save His people from their sins.'

So all this was done that it might be fulfilled which was spoken by the Lord through the prophet, saying: 'Behold, the virgin shall be with child, and bear a Son, and they shall call His name Immanuel,' which is translated, 'God with us.'

Then Joseph, being aroused from sleep, did as the angel of the Lord commanded him and took to him his wife, and did not know her till she had brought forth her firstborn Son. And he called His name Jesus.

II

Now after Jesus was born in Bethlehem of Judea in the days of Herod the king, behold, wise men from the East came to Jerusalem, saying, 'Where is He who has been born King of the Jews? For we have seen His star in the East and have come to worship Him.'

When Herod the king heard this, he was troubled, and all Jerusalem with him. And when he had gathered all the chief priests and scribes of the people together, he inquired of them where the Christ was to be born.

So they said to him, 'In Bethlehem of Judea, for thus it is written by the prophet:

But you, Bethlehem, in the land of Judah,
Are not the least among the rulers of Judah;
For out of you shall come a Ruler
Who will shepherd My people Israel.'

Then Herod, when he had secretly called the wise men, determined from them what time the star appeared. And he sent them to Bethlehem and said, 'Go and search carefully for the young Child, and when you have found Him, bring back word to me, that I may come and worship Him also.'

When they heard the king, they departed; and behold, the star which they had seen in the East went before them, till it came and stood over where the young Child was. When they saw the star, they rejoiced with exceedingly great joy. And when they had come into the house, they saw the young Child with Mary His mother, and fell down and worshipped Him. And when they had opened their treasures, they presented gifts to Him: gold, frankincense, and myrrh.

Then, being divinely warned in a dream that they should not return to Herod, they departed for their own country another way.

Now when they had departed, behold, an angel of the Lord appeared to Joseph in a dream, saying, 'Arise, take the young Child and His mother, flee to Egypt, and stay there until I bring you word; for Herod will seek the young Child to destroy Him.'

When he arose, he took the young Child and His mother by night and departed for Egypt, and was there until the death of Herod, that it might be fulfilled which was spoken by the Lord through the prophet, saying, 'Out of Egypt I called My Son.'

Then Herod, when he saw that he was deceived by the wise men, was exceedingly angry; and he sent forth and put to death all the male children who were in Bethlehem and in all its districts, from two years old and under, according to the time which he had determined from the wise men. Then was fulfilled what was spoken by Jeremiah the prophet, saying:

A voice was heard in Ramah,
Lamentation, weeping, and great mourning,
Rachel weeping for her children,
Refusing to be comforted,

Because they are no more.

Now when Herod was dead, behold, an angel of the Lord appeared in a dream to Joseph in Egypt, saying, 'Arise, take the young Child and His mother, and go to the land of Israel, for those who sought the young Child's life are dead.' Then he arose, took the young Child and His mother, and came into the land of Israel.

But when he heard that Archelaus was reigning over Judea instead of his father Herod, he was afraid to go there. And being warned by God in a dream, he turned aside into the region of Galilee. And he came and dwelt in a city called Nazareth, that it might be fulfilled which was spoken by the prophets, 'He shall be called a Nazarene' (Matthew 1:17 – 2:23).

2. How the birth stories differ

No question about it: these are two very different accounts of the birth of Jesus. However, they have generally been conflated in the Church's liturgical tradition with little regard for the differences between them. The birth stories were combined, as if it were the most natural thing in the world, into a single harmonious sequence in which one text perfectly complemented the other. Luke adds what is missing in Matthew, and if Luke fails to relate something, Matthew steps in, the result being a supposedly stable and consolidated whole.

Christmas Oratorios: Heinrich Schütz and Johann Sebastian Bach

The two most famous Christmas compositions in the history of German music do exactly this, sealing a harmonious image of Jesus' birth to the present day. Thus **Heinrich Schütz** (1585–1672) sticks very closely to the text of Luke's Gospel (2:1–21) at the beginning of his 1664 *Christmas Story* (a late work by the most important 17th-century composer of the Protestant German-speaking lands). This includes the announcement of the census, Mary and Joseph's peregrinations from Nazareth to Bethlehem, the Nativity, the appearance of the angel to the shepherds, the Adoration of the Shepherds, and the infant Jesus' circumcision and naming. Matthew's text (2:1–23) follows on from this quite organically: the appearance of the 'Wise Men from the East' at Herod's court, the Adoration of the Magi, the Flight into Egypt and the return to Nazareth after Herod's death. The compilation is rounded off by a combination of later quotations from Luke's Gospel (although in the meantime Luke has embarked on a completely different story): 'And Jesus increased in wisdom and stature, and in favour with God and men' (Luke 1:18; 2:52).

Johann Sebastian Bach (1685–1750) did something similar seventy years after Schütz. In his *Christmas Oratorio* (composed towards the end of 1734), the Cantor of St. Thomas's Church in Leipzig initially followed the order determined by the Church. Six holy days and Sundays needed arrangements, and Bach delivered six cantatas, especially since a separate Sunday occurred after New Year's Day in 1735. The composer was presented with the following readings for those six services:

First Day of Christmas: Birth and Annunciation to the
    Shepherds: Luke 2:1–14
Second Day of Christmas: The Adoration of the
    Shepherds: Luke 2:15–20
Third Day of Christmas: Prologue to the Gospel of
    John: John 1:1–14
New Year's Day: Circumcision and Naming of Jesus:
    Luke 2:21
First Sunday in the New Year: The Flight into Egypt:
    Matt. 2:13–23
Epiphany (6th January): The Coming and Adoration of
    the Magi: Matt. 2:1–12

Bach took a few liberties with the order of events in order to forge a logical narrative. The Flight into Egypt can hardly have taken place before the Adoration of the Magi, and the prologue to John's Gospel about the word of God made flesh has nothing to do with the stories of the Nativity in Bethlehem: it belongs to a different realm. So for the purposes of his oratorio Bach decided to leave out the official readings for the third day of Christmas and the first Sunday in the New Year, and to strike a compromise between the liturgical demands of his Church and the musical and textual requirements of his oratorio.

The advantage of this was that by combining Luke and Matthew, his six cantatas (as in Schütz) now followed a plausible chronology. Parts I to IV were taken from Luke 2:1 and 3–21, and Parts V and VI from Matt. 2:1–6 and 2:7–12 respectively. The disadvantage was that it is impossible for the audience of Bach's *Christmas Oratorio* to identify the differences – let alone certain contradictions – between the versions. Many people are still not aware, even today, that the accounts of Matthew and Luke are in many details 'not only different but incompatible'[12] – which makes a precise comparative examination of the two passages all the more compelling.

Different settings

There are already differences between the stories' settings. Matthew does not name the site of the angel's appearance to Joseph (Matt. 1). There then follows a brief mention of Bethlehem as the birthplace of Jesus, and Jerusalem as the seat of King Herod, who comes under pressure from the astrologers (Matt. 2:1–12) before the action shifts to Egypt (Matt. 2:13–15) and then Nazareth comes into view. The order of the scenes in Matthew is therefore: the angel's appearance to Joseph (unlocated) – Bethlehem – Jerusalem – Egypt – Nazareth.

In Luke, on the other hand, the settings are far clearer. Initially, everything takes place in Jerusalem, where an 'angel of the Lord' appears to the priest Zachariah in the temple (Luke 1:11); then the focus moves to the home of Zachariah and Elizabeth in the Jerusalem area, later referred to as being in 'the hill country [...] a city of Judah' (Luke 1:39), before we are told of the angel's appearance to Mary in Nazareth. This is followed by Mary's journey from Nazareth to Elizabeth's home and her return to Nazareth. From there the census prompts a journey to Bethlehem, then comes the birth of Jesus, and after the birth a journey to the temple in Jerusalem. Lastly there is the return to Nazareth. Hence, the order of the places mentioned by Luke is: Jerusalem – hills of Judah – Nazareth – hills of Judah – Nazareth – Bethlehem – Jerusalem – Nazareth.

The differences between the two gospels in terms of the locations could hardly be greater.

Different chronology

What about the chronology? The only thing the two Evangelists have in common here (Matt. 2:1; Luke 1:5) is the fact that Jesus must have been born during the lifetime of Herod the Great (ca. 73–4 BC). This confronts us (due to centuries of dependence on old calendar calculations) with the curious fact that Jesus of Nazareth must have been born in a year 'before Christ'.

More important, though, is the fact that neither Evangelist mentions a precise period (the season) or even a precise time (the year or day), which explains the problem the ancient Church faced in fixing a date for celebrations of Jesus' birth (25 December/6 January).[13] The Western Church only decided on the 25th of December as the feast of the birth of Jesus during Emperor Constantine's rule in the fourth century: it is first mentioned in a Roman calendar for the year 334! Scholars are divided as to why 25 December was chosen. The only consensus is that astronomical calculations fixed the winter solstice on that day. Driven by a need to set a separate feast for the birth of Jesus, Christians chose this particular date because Christ was regarded as the 'true sun' or the 'sun of justice'. This means that the roots of the feast of Jesus' birth were not pagan (for instance, to replace a feast of the sun god Sol Invictus) but purely astronomical and symbolic. St Augustine, for example, called 25 December the shortest day of the year, the point from which light once more begins to increase. It is the 'birth of the day'![14] Most Eastern Christians, however, celebrate Christ's birth or coming on 6 January, a date that is, not coincidentally, named 'Epiphany' – the 'appearance' of the Lord. According to the Father of the Church Clement of Alexandria in the second century AD, other Eastern congregations marked the event on 21 April or 20 May.

A close reading of the texts leads to the conclusion that Matthew is hazy about the chronology of events. The only thing he seems to establish beyond doubt is that the angel's appearance to Joseph (Matt. 1) clearly takes place nine months before Jesus' birth. After the birth, heeding a new appearance from the angel, Joseph sets off for Egypt, where he remains 'until the death of Herod'. No further details are provided. After Herod's death Joseph moves to Nazareth with his wife and child following another appearance by an angel. The offhand mention in Matt. 2:23 that Joseph 'dwelt in a city called Nazareth' (this too only in response to another order from God in a dream) suggests that the parents of Jesus cannot have been familiar with Nazareth. The period Matthew allows for all these events, from the angel's annunciation to the move to Nazareth, must encompass several years.

This is not the case in Luke. It is true that his external chronology, including indications of historical figures (the contemporaneity of Emperor Augustus, Herod the Great and Quirinius: Luke 2:1), entangles us in irreconcilable historical problems. According to the historical sources at our disposal, Quirinius was only appointed legate of Syria in 6 AD, by which time Herod was no more and Jesus very much alive. Also, there are no extant non-Christian sources to prove that Emperor Augustus (37 BC – 14 AD) ordered an empire-wide campaign of tax collection during this period. Hence we are unable to reconcile, from a historical perspective, Luke's attempted parallel timing of Jesus being born while Herod was king and Quirinius was conducting a census. Yet the internal chronology of Luke's account is utterly precise and transparent. This proceeds from the intertwining of the narrative with the account of the birth of John the Baptist. Then

Jesus is circumcised eight days after his birth (Luke 2:21). Forty days later, Mary undergoes her purification in the temple in Jerusalem according to the law of Moses (Luke 2:22–24) before immediately returning to Nazareth (Luke 2:39).

The conclusion is that it is not only on individual points of geography and chronology that the texts of the Gospels diverge or even contradict each other:

- Only **Luke** tells of Jesus' circumcision and a visit to the temple in Jerusalem. There is no mention of this in **Matthew**, which is why he has no knowledge either of the infant's meeting with an old man named Simeon (Luke 2:25–32) and a prophet by the name of Anna (Luke 2:36–38).
- In **Luke**, Mary and Joseph are living in Nazareth before the birth of their child (Luke 1:26) and therefore quite naturally return to the city afterwards (Luke 2:39). In **Matthew**, Nazareth only becomes relevant after the birth of Jesus.
- In **Matthew**, the Flight into Egypt takes place immediately after the birth and the Adoration of the Magi, whereas in **Luke** there is the Adoration of the Shepherds, followed by the circumcision and purification in the temple in Jerusalem. Both versions cannot be true.
- Whereas the entire process occurs within a recognisable time frame of some 16 months in **Luke**

(Jesus is conceived in the sixth month of Elizabeth's pregnancy, nine months later he is born
in Bethlehem, 'eight days' later he is circumcised
and after a few weeks his mother is purified in
the temple), **Matthew** allows a period of several
years. Here too, both versions cannot be true.

The differing roles of John the Baptist

There are also significant differences in composition and
structure between Matthew's and Luke's Gospels, and
this has ramifications for the two texts' theological profile.

Specifically, this means that Matthew puts Jesus' genealogy at the very beginning of his Nativity story (Matt.
1:1–17), while Luke relegates it to the end, shortly before
Jesus' first public appearance at the age of 30 (Luke 3:23–
38). While Matthew, as a Jewish Christian, is interested
in linking Jesus to the main bearers of God's promises to
Israel, i.e. with Abraham and David and David's descendants, Luke, as a Gentile Christian, is noticeably more uni-
versalist. He makes no mention of Abraham, but instead
traces Jesus' ancestry back to Adam and thus to God
himself (Luke 2:23–38). Whereas Matthew describes Jesus
as the son of Abraham and the son of David, for Luke he is
Adam's descendant and, like Adam, he is founding a new
human race at God's behest alone (with no earthly father).
Jesus, the son of Adam! We shall encounter this important
motif in a different form in the Qur'an (Sura 3:59–64).

It is a similar story regarding the accounts of John the Baptist, the son of Zachariah and Elizabeth, whom we shall meet again in the Qur'an. Luke structures his account very differently from Matthew. He alone has a separate birth story for John, and he deliberately places it before that of Jesus, linking the two stories through the figures of Mary and Elizabeth, and then giving John's father Zachariah a major role as the mouthpiece for a hymn that is a very precise theological and liturgical composition (Luke 1:67–79). Furthermore, after the birth of Jesus, Luke switches his focus back to the Baptist with an account of his public appearance (Luke 3:1–22).

Matthew, on the other hand, omits any account of John's birth. For him, John the Baptist only becomes interesting just before the public appearance of Jesus, in a short scene (Matt. 3:1–17) that simply presents John in contrast to Jesus, with no details of his subsequent fate (Luke 3:19–20) – purely as a forerunner, destined to be outdone by one mightier than he, who, unlike John, 'will baptise you with the Holy Spirit and fire' (Matt. 3:11; cf. Luke 3:16).

Differing versions of the birth of Jesus

There are also substantial differences regarding the birth itself, which the Qur'an will interpret after its own fashion. After presenting Jesus' genealogy, Matthew comes straight to the point, without further transition or preliminaries. It would be almost impossible to set the pre-natal scene more succinctly: 'After His mother Mary was betrothed to Joseph, before they came together, she was found with child of the Holy Spirit …' (Matt. 1:18).

Luke, on the other hand, develops the narrative very differently, giving the reader more information. In his version, the angel does not remain anonymous but has a name – Gabriel. In his version, the angel appears not to Joseph (as is consistently the case in Matthew) but only to Mary. In his version, the spot where the angel and Mary meet is not left unnamed but specifically described as a city of Galilee named Nazareth. His version focuses entirely on Mary: she is told of her distinction and the greatness of her future son, and her reaction is shown ('How can this be, since I do not know a man?', Luke 1:34).

Not a word here about the aspect in which Matthew is most interested. Matthew immediately allows his angel to address the social issue, as he knows that an unmarried woman with child would cause outrage. Joseph's mind must be put to rest – by divine intervention, as it were. 'Do not be afraid to take to you Mary, your wife, for that which is conceived in her is of the Holy Spirit' (Matt. 1:20). Matthew also realises that the explanations of spiritual conception and virgin birth are socially sensitive. This obstacle must therefore be 'theocentrically' removed, i.e. by divine intervention. Luke obviously sees no need for an intervention to prevent a social scandal. He doesn't resort to the same tactics as Matthew. The idea that the impossible is about to happen remains a secret shared only by the angel and Mary (Luke 1:34). So whereas Matthew tells the story entirely from the man's public perspective, Luke tells it entirely from the woman's private perspective: the point of view could hardly be more different.

The Nativity is handled much the same way. Matthew is clearly not aware of the things that Luke reports, and his story is about as prosaic and sober as could be, without any of the legendary dimension one might anticipate. Matthew tersely assumes that Jesus has already been born. Straight after the scene with the angel and Joseph – which obviously takes place at night in a dream (Matt. 1:20–25) – he devotes a single, factual sentence to the birth and immediately pivots to the astrologers' visit to Jerusalem:

> Now after Jesus was born in Bethlehem of Judea in the days of Herod the king, behold, wise men from the East came to Jerusalem, saying 'Where is he who has been born King of the Jews? For we have seen his star in the East and have come to worship Him' (Matt. 2:1–2).

Matthew would be hard pressed to mention the birth in Bethlehem any more casually. He then immediately shifts from the astrologers to the figure of King Herod, to whom he devotes an extraordinary amount of attention, detailing his summoning of the high priests and scholars, his audience with the astrologers, his feigned interest in the infant, his deceiving by the astrologers, and the slaughter of the innocents in Bethlehem.

In *theological* terms, Matthew's introduction of the 'wise men from the East' is obviously an attempt to incorporate messianic promises about the Gentiles' adoration of Israel's Messiah. In *compositional* terms, the Herod episode serves to prepare for the flight into Egypt, since there is a theological 'need' for this flight to fulfil a prophecy, namely the words of the prophet Hosea: 'When Israel was a child, I loved him, and out of Egypt I called My son' (Hos. 11:1; Matt. 2:15). Jesus, 'the son of God' and 'a new Moses', must, as heir to the old Moses, come 'out of Egypt'. The parallels between Moses and Jesus are very striking. The book of Exodus says:

'Go, return to Egypt; for all the men who sought your life are dead.' Then Moses took his wife and his sons … (Ex. 4:19–20)

The Gospel according to Matthew states:

But when Herod was dead, behold, an angel of the Lord appeared in a dream to Joseph in Israel, saying 'Arise, take the young Child and His mother, and go to the land of Israel, for those who sought the young Child's life are dead.' Then he arose, took the young

Child and His mother and came into the land of Israel (Matt. 2:19–21).

Luke, however, focuses exclusively on the Bethlehem tradition. He alone mentions a census under Emperor Augustus, the prime reason for Mary and Joseph travelling 'into Judea, to the city of David, which is called Bethlehem' (Luke 2:4). Luke alone knows the place and circumstances of the birth in Bethlehem: 'in a manger, because there was no room for them at the inn' (Luke 2:7). He alone knows about an angel appearing to the shepherds by night near Bethlehem and the shepherds' adoration of the baby Jesus (Luke 2:8–20). He alone knows about events in the temple in Jerusalem with Simeon and Anna after the birth. It is almost impossible to merge these two very different traditions into one coherent story. Inn, manger, shepherds, circumcision and visit to the temple? Not a word of these in Matthew. Conversely, Luke says nothing about the wise men's visit, the flight into Egypt and the massacre of the innocents in Bethlehem.

3. The primary message

And yet, despite all these varying and sometimes contradictory details, the two New Testament stories of the birth of Jesus are remarkably similar when it comes to the primary theological and social message.

Nothing is impossible for God

The birth of Jesus marks the beginning of a new initiative by God, ushering in a new era of liberation, redemption and forgiveness of sins. Heaven has, in a sense, become more porous, more porous in any case than before – as porous as it was in Abraham's time when angels also used to pass in and out, and an old woman like Sarah became fertile. Elizabeth can be recognised as a Sarah figure, and Zachariah as an Abraham figure (see Gen 18:11). There is a spirit of renewal in this latter-day Israel, the same spirit that reigned back in the age of their distant ancestors. It is not by chance that the key statement in Luke's description of the Annunciation to Mary is a quotation from the corresponding story of Abraham and Sarah, and what is striking in both cases is that the words are pronounced by an angel: 'For with God, nothing will be impossible' (Luke 1:37) and 'Is anything too hard for the Lord?' (Gen. 18:14).

Mary is therefore the latest in a line of Jewish mothers whom God treats in surprising fashion, liberating them from long childlessness by miraculously restoring their fertility. Women who come to mind are Isaac's wife, Rebecca (Gen. 25:21–24), Jacob's wives Leah and Rachel (Gen. 29:31 and 30:2) and also Hannah, the mother of the prophet Samuel (1 Sam. 1:1–20). Nor should we forget the story of the man who delivered Israel from the hands of the Philistines, Samson, whose mother was at first barren before an angel appeared with a message for her too: 'Indeed now you are barren and have borne no children, but you shall conceive and bear a son [...] And no razor shall come upon his head, for the child shall be a Nazirite to God from the womb' (Judges 13:3–5). Last but not least, there is Ishmael, whose mother Hagar was also granted an angelic apparition: 'Behold, you are with child, and you shall bear a son. You shall call his name Ishmael, because the Lord has heard your affliction' (Gen. 16:11). In all cases God gives an awe-inspiring sign to women whose age either prevented them from having more children, or who had never had children in the first place: 'For with God, nothing will be impossible ...'

Jesus' coming has made heaven more porous, and in the Nativity stories we see:

- *Angels* entering and leaving heaven as God's messengers. They are figures who interpret and direct events;
- *Signs* appearing in the sky: angels to the shepherds in the fields, and the star to the Magi en route to Bethlehem;
- *Nocturnal dreams* also play an important role. In Matthew, the angel only ever appears to Joseph by night in a dream; in Luke, the angel's appearance to the shepherds also occurs at night. The shepherds set out 'by night' to find Mary, Joseph and the babe in the manger. Joseph sets out for Egypt at night. Nocturnal dreams are also a medium for

encounters between the divine and the human in the New Testament.

Disruption: the power of the spirit of God

The fact that it is God who has initiated these events is demonstrated in particular by his disruption of the natural course of a human birth, especially in Jesus' case. This is what distinguishes the Nazarene from Isaac, Joseph and his brothers, from Samuel, Samson and Ishmael, as both Evangelists are seeking to emphasise that it is God's spirit rather than a human being that conceives this child. It is God's might that was and is operating here, not male virility, and they therefore highlight the disruptive nature of this event. Here, it is not human history and human physique that count; it is the spirit of God and the power of God, as illustrated by the angel's words to Mary in Luke's Gospel:

> The Holy Spirit will come upon you,
> and the power of the Highest will overshadow you;
> therefore, also, that Holy One who is born
> is to be called the Son of God.
> Now indeed, Elizabeth your relative
> has also conceived a son in her old age;
> and this is now the sixth month
> for her who was called barren.
> For with God nothing will be impossible (Luke 1:35–37).

This is the theocentric point of the two birth stories. What is misleadingly called the 'virgin birth' (as if the issue were merely a woman's biological virginity) is, to give it its precise theological title, 'conception by the spirit' or 'creation by the spirit'. The crucial factor here (and also later, for our understanding of the corresponding state-ments in the Qur'an) is that 'how' this conception by the Holy Spirit comes about is never stated, let alone described. This is the difference between the New Testa-ment and ancient mythology. We can safely assume that mythological accounts of intercourse between a god and a woman were common knowledge when the New Tes-tament accounts of Jesus' birth were written:

- *Heracles* was born of the union of Zeus and Alcmene;
- *Perseus* was born of the union of Zeus and Danaë;
- *Romulus* and *Remus* were born of the union of Mars and Rhea.

Similar stories of divine/human procreation are also told of the great figures of antiquity, both rulers such as Alexander the Great and Augustus as well as philosophers like Plato and Pythagoras.

However, Matthew and Luke do not have a pagan, mythological vision of the conception, but rather a Jewish pneumatological one. God's spirit (*pneuma* in Greek) is the sole power at work here. This preserves God's transcendence in the midst of immanence. Therefore the two essential statements of Luke's Gospel are extraordinarily modest, almost chaste, but that does not make them any less definite. Luke 1:35 reads:

The Holy Spirit will come upon you.
The power of the Highest will overshadow you.

In the exegesis of the Tübingen-based New Testament scholar Peter Stuhlmacher, this means that just as 'the earth was without form, and void; and darkness was on the face of the deep. And the Spirit of God was hovering over the face of the waters' (Gen. 1:2; see also Psalm 33:6), the same now applies to Mary. Also, just as the tabernacle (the model for the temple in Jerusalem) was overshadowed by the cloud of God's presence (Ex. 40:35), the same now applies to Mary. She will be affected by the creative power of the one and only God, who calls the non-existent into being with his awe-inspiring breath (see Rom. 4:17).[15] Creation theology therefore defines the manner in which the story of Jesus' birth is told. 'Creation out of nothing' is emphasised here. God is at work – the God who, according to Paul in his letter to the Romans, 'gives life to the dead and calls those things which do not exist as though they did' (Rom. 4:17).

Luke 1:35 therefore refers back to the very beginning of creation. Adam and Jesus mirror each other. Old creation versus new creation. Old man versus new man. Now we can see why Luke traces Jesus' genealogy back to Adam: Adam is the first creature; Jesus, son of Adam, is the last in a long line of God's creations (Luke 3:38).

So both Adam and Jesus were created by the word of God alone. 'Just as the creation stories are attempts to interpret the secret of the world as stemming from God,' writes the Catholic New Testament scholar Hubert Frankemölle, who teaches in Paderborn, Germany, 'the story of the virgin birth should be interpreted as a religious explanation for the belief that Jesus – like Adam and Immanuel in Isa. 7:14 – owes his existence and conception entirely to the creative effect of the spirit of God. This is valid, even though the parallels are not entirely consistent, since neither virgin birth nor conception by the spirit are mentioned in the creation of Adam, nor is there any talk of spiritual conception when Immanuel is born of a virgin in Isa. 7:14. However, the life-giving creative power of God is assumed in both cases.'[16] We will look at the corresponding statements in the Qur'an in Sura 3:59–64 (see Chapter V, 1–2).

Hence there is a sense of a fresh departure and a new beginning about the New Testament birth stories. The Jesuit Friedrich Spee von Langenfeld (1591–1635), a brave opponent of trials for witchcraft and also a great poet, captured this atmosphere in a Christmas hymn, written in 1622 and containing three verses full of rich imagery. He gave a wonderfully harmonious interpretation of this dimension of the New Testament birth stories in the language of the late Baroque:

O Saviour, rend the heavens wide;
Come down, come down with mighty stride.
Unlock the gates, the doors break down;
Unbar the way to heaven's crown.

O Father, dew from heaven send;
As gentle dew, O Son, descend.
Drop down, you clouds, and torrents bring:
To Jacob's line rain down the King.

O earth, in flowering bud be seen;
Clothe hill and dale in garb of green.
O earth bring forth this Blossom rare;
O Saviour, rise from meadow fair.[17]

Let us just call these images to mind again and repeat this powerful language to ourselves. As 'Saviour', Jesus is to 'rend' the heavens and 'break down' the gates of heaven. The clouds are to 'drop down' and 'rain down' the heaven-sent saviour. Humankind longs for one who will make the earth flower again so that hill and dale are dressed 'in garb of green'. It would be difficult to verbalise the spirit of messianic regeneration caused by Jesus' birth any more sensually than through such expressive, dynamic verbs as 'rend', 'descend', 'rain down', 'drop down', 'bring forth' and 'rise'.

A signal to Israel and the Gentiles

The powerful spiritual message that God made visible
through the birth of Jesus is aimed first and foremost at
his people of Israel but then to the Gentiles beyond Israel.
The new-born baby is Israel's Messiah, long awaited and
finally come: neither text admits the faintest doubt here.
Indeed, they strive, through a tight web of textual interpre-
tative signals, to transform this belief into undeniable fact.
This is why the words of the prophets play such a major
part in both accounts, be it Isaiah on the subject of the
young woman who will conceive a child (Matt. 1:25: Isa.
7:14); the prophet Micah about Bethlehem, the ancient
town of David and the Messiah (Matt. 2:5–6; Mic. 5:1); the
prophet Hosea about Egypt (Matt. 2:15; Hos. 11:1); or the
prophet Jeremiah about the slaughter of the Innocents in
Bethlehem (Matt. 2:16–18; Jer. 31:15).

Matthew is particularly intent on embedding Jesus'
coming in the story of the people of Israel and their messianic expectations. This explains the genealogy at the
beginning of his Gospel, which deliberately presents Jesus
Christ as 'the son of David, the son of Abraham' (Matt.
1:1). The inclusion of the Egypt scene is of special theological and symbolic importance, as we have seen. Just
as the old Moses came from Egypt, so the new Moses,
Jesus, will come from Egypt too. This signals that the birth
of Jesus is the start of a new exodus by the people of Israel
– not from physical slavery as before, but this time from
spiritual and moral enslavement, decline and blindness:

> And she will bring forth a Son, and you shall call His
> name Jesus, for He will save His people from their sins
> (Matt. 1:21).

Yet God's plans also concern the Gentile peoples beyond Israel; here too the two Evangelists leave no room for doubt. They both know that it has proved impossible to convert the whole of Israel, which is why the Adoration of the Magi is so important to Matthew from the very start. Non-Jews 'from the East', representatives of pagan peoples, worship Jesus, while 'all Jerusalem' is troubled at first and then either rejects Jesus' Messiahship or plots to murder the new-born baby. The later Christian tradition upgrading the Eastern astrologers to 'kings' stems from the fact that Matthew's description (in 2:11) of the astrologers' gifts to Jesus (gold, frankincense and myrrh) alludes to chapter 60 of the Book of Isaiah: 'The Gentiles shall come to your light, and kings to the brightness of your rising' (Isa. 60:3) and, only a few lines later in the same chapter: 'All [...] shall bring gold and incense, and they shall proclaim the praises of the Lord' (Isa .60:6; Matt. 2:11). This quotation also explains the later triad of supposed 'kings', although Matthew does not mention a number (see Matt. 2:1). This triad is quite obviously inferred from the number of gifts Matthew lists – 'gold, frankincense and myrrh' – since it is presumed that a separate visitor presents each gift.

What about Luke? In view of his intended audience

(non-Jews) he stresses Jesus' significance not only to Israel but also to the Gentiles, if anything in even starker terms than Matthew does. Luke sets up this dual perspective, bit by bit, by having skilfully composed hymns spoken by Mary ('My soul magnifies the Lord', Luke 1:46–55), Zachariah ('Blessed is the Lord God of Israel!', Luke 1:68–79) and Simeon ('Lord, now You are letting Your servant depart in peace', Luke 2:29–32). It says in Mary's 'Magnificat' that with the coming of Jesus, God has helped 'his servant' and has shown 'His mercy' as he promised to 'our fathers' and 'to Abraham and to his seed forever' (Luke 1:54–55). There is initially the same intra-Jewish perspective with Zachariah, who is after all a priest at the temple in Jerusalem. God has 'saved' Israel from its enemies, and he has not forgotten 'His holy covenant' and the 'oath' he swore to Abraham. Jesus will announce to 'His people' that there will be 'salvation', 'remission of sins' and the 'tender mercy of our God' (Luke 1:71–73; 77). Yet 'the Gentiles' are included as early as Simeon's canticle:

> Lord, now You are letting Your servant depart in
>   peace,
> According to Your word;
> For my eyes have seen Your salvation
> Which You have prepared before the face of all
>   peoples,
> A light to bring revelation to the Gentiles,
> And the glory of Your people Israel (Luke 2:29–32).

It follows that: *Alongside the theocentric perspective ('For with God nothing is impossible', Luke 1:37), the two Evangelists also present a Christ-centred message: Jesus is a sign of the spirit of God, 'the Messiah, the Lord' (Luke 2:11), 'the Son of the Highest', 'the Son of God' (Luke 1:32; 1:35). His coming heralds a new era. According to the New Testament accounts, the 'impossible' that God is now capable of is realised in Jesus, through Jesus and with Jesus, in a way that shatters theological and social ideas about God and the Messiah. It is truly unexpected that Israel's Messiah should come into the world as a baby in a manger.*

4. No world peace without world justice

A Messiah in the manger

Both Evangelists go to great lengths to emphasise the low-liness of Jesus the Messiah. This Son of God does not come into the world like the sons of pagan gods, in gran-deur and power, but – and Luke, in particular, stresses this – in humility and lowliness. There's nothing romantic about his description. Luke doesn't idealise the poverty of the inn and the manger; he simply reports soberly and almost casually on the situation: the circumstances of their journey left Mary and Joseph no choice (Luke 2:7). Nor are they portrayed as representatives of the 'poor', as later clichés would have it. Luke says nothing to suggest that Mary and Joseph are socially 'poor'. Indeed, this seems highly unlikely reading Matthew, as he later mentions Joseph's 'solid' trade as a 'carpenter' (see Matt. 13:55). It is therefore not through suggestions of Jesus' family actually being poor that Luke achieves the motif of poverty, but through the new-born baby's impact and appeal among the lower levels of society – a very different Israel to the one represented by the political and religious establishment.

But why choose shepherds as the audience? The history of exegesis has highlighted the fact that rabbinic Judaism vilified shepherds as a profession because they could not live up to the strict hygiene standards of the Torah. It is impossible to say whether this is why Luke casts shepherds here. It does, however, seem clear that the shepherds embody a different face of Israel, and that is why they hear the annunciation of the Messiah. It is no coincidence that the prophet Micah's words, interpreted as an announcement of the Messiah's coming, run as follows:

But you, Bethlehem Ephrathah,
Though you are little among the thousands of Judah;
Yet out of you shall come forth to Me
The One to be Ruler of Israel,
Whose goings forth are from of old,
From everlasting.
Therefore He shall give them up,

Until that time that she who is in labour has given
    birth;
Then the remnant of His brethren
Shall return to the children of Israel.
And He shall stand and feed His flock
In the strength of the Lord,
In the majesty of the name of the Lord His God;
And they shall abide,
For now He shall be great
To the ends of the earth;
And this one shall be peace (Mic. 5:1).

Hence Bethlehem is the city of David, the city of the Messiah. David was a shepherd and Israel a people of shepherds, and Micah 5:1 promises the Jewish people a messianic shepherd. He will come forth from David's birthplace (see 1 Sam. 20:6), the small town of Bethlehem in Judah, to protect God's chosen people from their enemies and usher in an age of peace for Israel. This is how Luke reports it.

Remarkably, Matthew does not express the lowliness motif in social terms either. In any case, the new-born child is not born in a manger, but in a normal dwelling: the astrologers find the infant, quite naturally, 'in a house' (Matt. 2:11). Matthew introduces the lowliness motif mainly via death, which acts, in compositional terms, as a symbolic prefiguring of Jesus' eventual fate. This is to emphasise that the 'Messiah' lives in the shadow of death from the very start. He is either threatened with death (murder by Herod) or the catalyst of death (the Massacre of the Innocents). From the outset, his life is one of lamentation and tears. Rachel's desolation as a mother, recorded in the quotation in Jeremiah (Matt. 2:18; Jer. 31:15), hovers over the scene: it prefigures the desolation of the grieving women at the Passion (see Matt. 27:55–56). What is striking too is that 'King of the Jews', the name used by the astrologers before Herod, is not repeated until the Passion (see Matt. 27:11 and 29.37). This expression underlines the contrast between the new-born and 'King' Herod. Structurally, therefore, the story of Jesus is bookended by death. There is no hint of a timeless myth here: the story is anchored in space and time.

What sets Jesus apart from Buddha and Lao-tzu

That is not true of every global religion. India? Whether the god Krishna has a date of birth is unimportant in view of the vast cycles the world undergoes (the destruction and rebirth of the cosmos). Whether Buddha was born in the Lumbini grove near Kapilavastu or somewhere else might be useful for modern-day Buddhism (as a pilgrimage site!), but it has no bearing on Buddhist teaching. Nobody has any idea where Lao-tzu was born, and it is meaningless to those who wish to discover and take the path of Tao. How about Confucius' birthplace? He was apparently born in the small old feudal city of Lu, close to modern Qufu (Shandong Province), but this fact is largely irrelevant to anyone wishing to follow the teachings in Confucius' 'conversations' about order.

Not so for the prophetic religions: Judaism, Christianity and Islam. History is important in these religions, and place and time play a defining role. The Israelites are God's chosen people, and he revealed his will to them through precise commandments. For a religion with Indian or Chinese origins, this thought is as absurd as the idea that the figure of Jesus or the descent of the Qur'an heralded the start of a new era, setting world history on a different course. What is history to someone who thinks in cosmic terms? Yet when it comes to the major prophetic figures of global religions – Moses, Jesus and Muhammad – where they come from and the fate that befalls them are all-important, for they say something about the 'fate' of God himself. This explains why Luke's story of Jesus' birth has a definite outcome and a precise geographical location.

Roman domination seen from Bethlehem

So definite and so precise, in fact, that a close reading of the texts reveals a remarkable gift for storytelling. Both Evangelists deserve to be taken seriously as 'authors' (Walter Jens).[18] Luke's account of the birth opens in the very first line with a sweeping panorama: 'And it came to pass in those days that a decree went out from Caesar Augustus …' (Luke 2:1). The keywords are:

- *Politics:* Rome, Caesar Augustus
- *Economics:* registration, general census
- *Demographics:* an empire-wide census. 'All the world' is to be registered.

So this evangelist takes a global perspective, starting with the imperial capital, Rome, then zooming in on the province of Syria, the district of Galilee and ending up in a little town called Bethlehem. Rome – Syria – Galilee – Bethlehem: the focus is ever closer, the detail ever sharper.

We can conclude the following:

The storyteller's 'cinematography' moves from global to local. Rome – Syria – Galilee – Bethlehem with its stable and manger: that is the 'panning' motion. Taken in reverse, these signals seek to make clear that what happens in this stable has an impact on Bethlehem, Galilee, Syria and Rome. What happens on this night affects the whole world, and that is intentional. The discrepancy is still grotesque: Caesar in Rome, his governor in Syria – and the new-born baby in the manger of a packed inn.

So this descent is actually coupled with an ascent. The downward motion from Caesar to babe in a manger, and from the palace in Rome to the stable in Bethlehem in the second half of Luke's text represents a no less skilfully and dramatically 'constructed' upward motion, from the manger, the lowliest of the low, to the heights of the angel's appearance; from bottom to top. Now the decisive message can be delivered. It is delivered 'from on high' to a world cowering in fear – a message of non-fear and the great joy of the Messiah's coming. It must be delivered 'from on high', since the world, under Roman domination, is hardly capable of such a message on its own. It must also be delivered 'from on high' because the entire process depends on a child, 'wrapped in swaddling cloths, lying in a manger'. A whole host of angels must be mobilised to convert this fragile beginning into a credible message:

Glory to God in the highest,
And on earth peace, goodwill toward men!

In a sense, the curtain is pulled aside for a second, and God's world laid bare. The angels represent God's descent to earth. They tell of God's glory and peace and God's peace for all men, meaning a peace that is different from any that exists in the real world. Let us not forget that when Luke recorded his account of the Nativity, he and his contemporaries could already look back on the Jewish war, the fall of Jerusalem and the Romans' destruction of the temple in 70 BC. In a sense, Luke reopens this whole tragic chapter when he mentions Caesar Augustus at its very beginning. It had all begun with Augustus (who was emperor from 37 BC to 14 AD). At the time of Jesus' birth he was regarded as an emperor of peace. The Pax Romana was principally a Pax Augustana. Shortly after his death in 14 AD, Augustus was already being worshipped as a son of the god Apollo, and myths about the birth of the 'divine Augustus' and legends of his father Octavianus abounded.

Yet the Pax Romana was based on the power of the Roman legions, a presence that was keenly felt by the Jews in Palestine. In practical terms, Roman-style peace equated to military occupation. The announcement by the 'emperor of peace' that everyone should 'register' (meaning a census for the purposes of taxation) led to terrorism, unrest and insecurity in Palestine. The introduction of Roman taxation triggered the founding of the Zealots' liberation movement, which paid a heavy price for rebelling against Rome in 66 AD. Israel was doomed, and Jerusalem and its temple were destroyed in 70 AD.

Luke's vision of peace incarnate in Bethlehem therefore had a double message, something that was abundantly clear to the evangelist himself and to his intended audience. It was directed at:

- The peace programme of Caesar Augustus, represented in Palestine by his vassal, King Herod the Great – a 'friend of Caesar', as a contemporary engraving tells us. This peace is based not on truth but on the power of boots on the ground and ultimately on lies, of which Herod was a perfect proponent;
- The fundamentalist Zealots, who had roused the people into a hopeless battle to the death against

the Roman legions. The price of rebelling with the
sword is to be destroyed by the sword. The price
of this kind of peace is the peace of the dead.

The Catholic New Testament scholar Rudolf Pesch gives
an impressive analysis of this political and social dimension of the Nativity story in his exegesis of the Christmas
Gospel: 'The legend of Jesus' birth indirectly but fairly
clearly targets "political theology", the ideology of Caesar's *raison d'état* and the social order associated with the
Roman emperor's policies; it also targets the ideology of
Jewish theocratic nationalism and zealotism. The legend
of the birth of Jesus steals Caesar's halo as the saviour of
peace by reminding the reader of the "registration", which
brought oppression and provoked a warlike rebellion. It
countered Jewish national expectation, which was still
searching for a liberating Messiah, with the message of the
peace of Christ, who had already brought the good tidings
of God's dominion to "all men", and who, as the Lord on
high, had already commenced his reign of peace.'[19]

Jerusalem's hegemony from the perspective of the babe in the manger

And Matthew? He too is an impressive literary stylist.
His Jerusalem scene skilfully reveals a triangular relationship and gives a sharp sense of dramatic contrast. The
astrologers arrive at a time of heightened political and

religious tension. They encounter the Jerusalem establishment comprising the political leader Herod and the religious leaders – the 'chief priests and scribes of the people' (Matt. 2:4). It is within this triangle that reactions to the news of the Messiah's birth play out: astrologers against high priests/scribes and Herod. For maximum effect the storyteller depicts the shock of 'all of Jerusalem'; no doubt a bold piece of rhetorical exaggeration. Yet it serves the point of the story: people in Jerusalem expected many things at the time, but not the birth of the Messiah, for this could have called the political and religious establishment's monopoly of power into question.

This is what makes Matthew's use of contrast so striking. 'All the chief priests and scribes' confirm, when asked, that Bethlehem is the birthplace of the Messiah (in accordance with the relevant passage in the book of the prophet Micah, 5:1), yet no official religious representative thinks to check when it comes to Jesus. It is not they who set out for Bethlehem to see for themselves but the astrologers, sent on their way by the potentate amid feigned interest. The scribes become Herod's accomplices! They confirm the prophecy, 'but show no emotion and thus have no intention of setting out themselves. Whereas the Jews show nothing but disinterest and hostility, the Magi travel from afar as representatives of Eastern wisdom and as the spiritual elite of the Gentiles.'[20]

To recap: *when we think about the birth of Jesus, we must keep in mind the political and economic situation of the time! From the perspective of the babe in the manger, there can be no lasting peace based purely on power, whether that be the power of money or the power of weapons. No world peace without world justice!*

To reflect on the meaning of Jesus' birth is therefore to reflect on the state of the world, in the light of the words of that great hymn of earthly justice that Luke the Evangelist very deliberately puts in the mouth of Mary, the mother of Jesus:

My soul magnifies the Lord,
 And my spirit has rejoiced in God my Saviour.
For He has regarded the lowly state of His
    maidservant;
For behold, henceforth all generations will call me
    blessed.
For He who is mighty has done great things for me,
And holy is His name.
And His mercy is on those who fear Him
From generation to generation.
He has shown strength with His arm;
He has scattered the proud in the imagination of their
    hearts.
He has put down the mighty from their thrones,
And exalted the lowly.
He has filled the hungry with good things,
And the rich He has sent away empty.
He has helped His servant Israel,

In remembrance of His mercy,
As He spoke to our fathers,
To Abraham and to his seed forever (Luke 1:46–55).

Through the lens of a close, parallel reading, the texts' fundamental message becomes ever clearer. 'The Christmas story,' writes Walter Jens, 'the best-known text in world literature, tilted this way and that, yet still constantly capable of turning up new and surprising facets, here cosmic and there melancholy. The Christmas story is a text, which, to cite Ernst Bloch, refuses to be left alone as unapproachable or to be subjugated to the here and now. It is, rather, an old text that needs to be transposed so that it touches and co-denotes the present day, whenever that may be. The Christmas story: a piece of prose that cannot be told in passing, but must be painted passionately, emotionally, subjectively, gently and angrily.'[21]

Thus the New Testament Christmas stories retain a challenging and politically charged message. Not historical criticism, but rather, as Hans Küng so accurately noted: 'Romantic, belittling idealisation and privatisation on the one hand, and superficial secularisation and busy commercialisation on the other have hollowed out the message of Christmas and its festivities. As if the "lovely curly-haired boy" – not in Luke and Matthew, but in pictures – were always smiling and did not wail with normal human misery (as indicated, without any hint of socio-critical protest, by the crib and the swaddling cloths)! As if the saviour of the destitute, born in a stable, were not clear evidence of an alignment with the nameless (the shepherds) against the powerful, who are referred to by name (Augustus, Quirinius)! As if the Magnificat enunciated by the blessed virgin did not announce in belligerent terms the reassessment of the prevailing hierarchy by putting down the mighty and exalting the lowly, feeding the hungry and neglecting the rich! As if the sweet Nativity led one to overlook his deeds and fate three decades later, along with the fact that the babe in the manger already bore the sign of the cross on his brow! As if – as later in his trial by a Jewish court – the annunciation scenes to Mary and the shepherds (in the middle of the Christmas story) did not express the community's perfect creed through the use of several titles (Son of God, Saviour, Messiah, King, Lord), and the fact that these titles were addressed not to the Roman emperor but to this child! As if instead of the illusory Pax Romana – bought with tax increases, military expansion, pressure on minorities and a poor economic outlook – the true Pax Christi were not being announced here with "great joy", based on a new order of human relations under the banner of God's philanthropy and fraternity between all people!'[22]

PART TWO

The Birth of Muhammad

Concerning Mohammed's birth miraculous things are related, such as were told earlier concerning the births of Moses, Buddha, Alexander, Jesus, Mary, and many others. In the hour of his birth a brilliant light shone over the entire world from East to West. With miraculous clairvoyance Amina saw the palaces of Syria and the necks of the camels in Busrah. When Mohammed was born he fell to the ground, took a handful of earth, and gazed toward heaven. He was born clean and without a spot, as a lamb is born, circumcised, and with the navel-cord already cut.[23]

Tor Andræ, *Mohammed: The Man and His Faith* (1932)

A Turkish dervish of the seventeenth century sings: 'The night in which the Messenger was born is without doubt similar to the Night of Might', that is the night in which the Koran was revealed for the first time, which is called in Sura 97 'better than a thousand months'. [...] This [...] clearly indicate[s] the degree to which veneration of the Prophet had increased during the late Middle Ages.

Annemarie Schimmel, *And Muhammad is His Messenger* (1981)[24]

How are we to employ the elements presented above to pursue a dialogue with Muslims? We have tried to give an intellectually rigorous and precise reading of the two New Testament accounts of the Nativity, and to present the concordance of the two stories' basic messages as well as their divergences and contradictions on points of detail.

1. How Muslims read the New Testament

The texts themselves call for such close reading. They are human testimonies of faith. They seek to understand the birth of Jesus from the point of view of God's historic bond with Israel. By doing so they signal that these interpretations are in a 'state of flux', bearing the imprint of various experiences and guided by different accounts. For Christians these differences are part of the diversity of human experience, multiple perspectives on one and the same event. One can trust the message of these testimonies; in fact, one can hear 'God's word' to us humans in and through them, despite and due to the many divergences and contradictions in their details.

Muslims criticise Christian contradictions

What Christians see as an advantage, traditionally minded Muslims view as a weakness and a loss. This should be borne in mind when dialogue leads to encounters with such representatives of Islam. Muslims such as these will exploit any divergence and contradiction Christians present. They interpret the mere fact that there are *four* Gospels as a sign of the imperfection and corruption of Christian accounts. To them this confirms that the existing New Testament cannot be the 'Word of God', which is why there is a need for the Qur'an to re-establish the original perfection of God's revelatory scriptures!

According to a traditional reading of the Qur'an, God entrusted the Torah to the Jews and the Gospel to the Christians, but that Gospel (to stick with this example) is no longer identical to the one the Christians present as their 'Holy Scripture'. One only has to read a work of Muslim propaganda such as *Your Way to Islam* by Mohammad Suliman al-Ashqer (which I bought in January 2006 in the Muslim quarter of Jerusalem's old town) to find such thoughts expressed in their most unadulterated form. In Chapter 8, entitled 'Faith in Holy Scriptures' of this extremely widely distributed short text, it is explained as if it were the most obvious thing in the world that:

1. Allah has sent down to a number of Messengers, Books in order to proclaim them to mankind.
2. These Books contain the Words of Allah.
3. Among them are the Sheets of Ibrahim (Abraham), Taurat revealed to Moosa (Moses), Az-Zabour (psalms) revealed to Dawood (David), The Injil (Gospel) revealed to Isa (Jesus), And The Qur'an

sent down to Muhammad, (Peace be upon them all).

4. Jews and Christians distorted some parts of their Books (Taurat and Injil).

5. Being the last Book assuredly guarded from corruption, The Qur'an confirms the truth in the previous Books and guards it.

6. Whatever, in those Books, differs from The Qur'an is corrupted or abrogated.[25]

It is impossible to call this a contribution to a dialogue with Christians. This same 'method' is also employed by larger and more challenging publications (also on sale in the Muslim quarter of Jerusalem's old town) with titles such as *Stories of the Prophets* or *Prophethood and the Prophets*. Whereas *Stories of the Prophets* by Ibn Kathir, a well-known 14th-century historian, only documents texts from the Qur'an and the Sunna,[26] *Prophethood and the Prophets* by Al-Sheikh Muhammad Ali Sabuni also includes a commentary.[27] Any Jewish and Christian readers glad to find their own tradition discussed (in a long chapter about Adam, Abraham, Joseph, Noah, Jonah, Moses and Jesus) in a book intended for Muslim students, will feel alienated after reading it. References to the Torah and the Gospel are included purely to point out their contradictions and to refer back to the Qur'an. One example is the genealogy of Jesus. Matthew's and Luke's Gospels contain undeniably diverging and irreconcilable information, as we have already seen (Matt. 1:1–17; Luke 3:23–38). This Muslim exegete draws up exhaustive lists of examples:

1. Luke's Gospel says that Joseph is the son of Eli, whereas Matthew's Gospel says that Joseph is the son of Jacob.
2. Luke's Gospel says that he [Joseph] is the descendant of Nathan, the son of David, whereas Matthew's Gospel says that he is the descendant of Solomon, the son of David.
3. Luke's Gospel says that Jesus' forefathers were not rulers and were not famous, whereas Matthew's Gospel says that Jesus' forefathers were rulers and famous.
4. Luke's Gospel claims that there were 41 generations between Jesus and David, whereas Matthew's Gospel says that there were 28 generations between David and the Messiah.

We do not know how it is possible to reconcile these contradictions in a book that billions of Christians believe to be the word of God and the absolute truth. In Allah, there can be no explanation apart from that changes were made by religious leaders [at the time], as is confirmed in the Holy Qur'an.[28]

It continues in this vein on issues of Christology. Examples from the New Testament are cited in order to confirm

the Qur'an or to be rejected as mistaken. The same publication unambiguously claims:

> The Holy Gospel, which God revealed to his servant
> and prophet Jesus, the son of Mary, is not the one
> found among Christians today. As expressed in the
> Qur'an, their Gospel has been corrupted and changed.
> There are obvious contradictions in these Gospels.
> Furthermore, if God revealed only one Gospel, how
> did it become four Gospels? [...]
>
> The Messiah came to his companions with a book
> which was the Gospel but which was flouted by
> the people over time. As a result it was lost. Jesus'
> followers then relied on books written by Jesus'
> disciples and their disciples or others who came after
> them. The number of Gospels grew until there were
> more than a hundred of them. The Church stepped in
> to reject any Gospel that contradicted its guidelines,
> and it eventually only confirmed four Gospels, those
> known today, despite the obvious contradictions
> between them.[29]

The book's overall conclusion is therefore that the Qur'an
is the perfect, ultimate and conclusive word of God. It
was needed in order to correct the distortions, depravi-
ties, misunderstandings and contradictions of the Christian 'Holy' Book.

Contra the missionary propagandists

It requires little argument to prove that people who espouse this position are neither willing to engage in dialogue nor capable of doing so. The argumentation is based on self-immunisation and self-aggrandisement. It represents ideologically totalitarian propaganda rather than an open-minded approach to communication. It is not an expression of respect for other religious beliefs but a proclamation of contempt, superiority and arrogant conviction. Individual verses or passages from other holy books are singled out and rejected on the grounds of the authors' criteria of truth. This is what Christians did to Muslims for centuries (calling the Qur'an 'a book of lies'), and certain Muslims now treat the Christian tradition the same way.

Respect for the dignity and integrity of one another's holy books is the basis for all dialogue. This book presupposes that respect, urging and practising a different kind of dealings by Muslims with Christians and by Christians with Muslims. As the 'Joint Declaration' made in Tehran in May 2008 says:

> Generalisation should be avoided when speaking of religions. Differences of confessions within Christianity and Islam, diversity of historical contexts are important factors to be considered.
>
> Religious traditions cannot be judged on the basis of a single verse or a passage present in their

respective holy Books. A holistic vision as well as an adequate hermeneutical method is necessary for a fair understanding of them.

2. The origins of the Prophet

I have therefore absolutely no intention of criticising Muslims for the fact that over the course of history and in contradiction with the Qur'an, they have adapted the image of their Prophet very willingly to their own religious needs, desires and wishful thinking. Instead, I respectfully acknowledge that there is a gaping discrepancy between the image of the Prophet in the Qur'an and the image conveyed by Islamic religious history, and I would like to understand why. The accounts of the birth of the Prophet are a test case for me.

The first biography of the Prophet

The Qur'an is similar to most books in the New Testament in that it is not interested in the events surrounding the birth of the Prophet. Indeed, it does not even mention the birth – just as Mark's Gospel, the oldest, makes no mention of the birth of Jesus and famously begins with Jesus' first appearance in public: the baptism in the river Jordan. It is only then (and not at his birth) that the Nazarene is proclaimed the 'Son of God' (Mark 1:11).

The Qur'an is much the same. It is not the physical

birth of the Prophet that is decisive but the spiritual birth, not the human birth but the prophet's birth. The crucial issue is when and how Muhammad became the messenger of the One God. Sura 96 is seen as marking the beginning of the revelations to the Prophet in the year 610, by which time Muhammad was already 40 years old.

The situation had completely changed 150 years after the Prophet's death. Around the year 770 a man called Ibn Ishaq ('the son of Isaac') died in Baghdad. He came from Medina, where he had been born in 704. He left us the first comprehensive description of the life of the Prophet, indeed the very first comprehensive history of the Islamic world, which he probably wrote in Iraq in 750. A good 120 years separate his book from the historical Muhammad. The Gospels were written some 50–70 years after the historical Jesus.

It is no coincidence that a description of the life of the Prophet was written during this period. When Ibn Ishaq set down his text, Islam had spread from Spain to the Indus valley in a period of only 100 years – an expansion unrivalled in the history of religion. The Umayyad Caliphate (661–750 AD), based in Damascus, had already been succeeded by the Abbasid Caliphate (from 750, with Baghdad as its capital). Ibn Ishaq could therefore look back on the successful development of Islam, unprecedented in world history. This suggests that it had become politically desirable for someone to write a comprehensive, epic depiction of the life of the Prophet.

The book originally consisted of four parts. The first part began with the story of the creation of the world, moved on to the deeds of the great prophetic figures from Adam to Jesus, and proceeded to discuss the Arab tribes during the pre-Islamic era. The next two parts contained further details about the 'mission' and the 'struggles' of the Prophet. The fourth part continued the story of Islam until the historiographer's own lifetime.

It must be noted that the original and complete version of Ibn Ishaq's text has not survived. We owe the fact that some parts of it are available to an Egyptian scholar by the name of Ibn Hisham, who died circa 830 AD. One of Ibn Ishaq's pupils had brought him the book from Iraq, and the Egyptian crafted this material into the book we now know as *al-sira* (the 'biography') of the Prophet, which remains the most studied biography of Muhammad to this day. Yet Ibn Hisham's 'edition' extends the distance between the historical Muhammad and the first available biography to almost 200 years.

Miraculous signs during conception and pregnancy

The narrative treatment of the figure of Jesus in Christian congregations by Matthew and Luke was increasingly adopted by Muslim communities with regard to Muhammad, possibly as a response to, and in competition with, the Christian tradition. There was an obvious desire within Islam to rival Christianity. In any case, it is striking that the very first biography of the Prophet presents a genealogy. Ibn Ishaq opens his book every bit as deliberately as Mark the Evangelist with a genealogy, and no less deliberately traces Muhammad's ancestry back to Adam, as Luke had done. To quote selected passages of this genealogy verbatim:

> Muhammad is the son of Abdallah, the son of
> Abdalmuttalib, the son of Hashim [...] the son of
> Ismail, the son of Ibrahim [...] the son of Yard, the son
> of Mahlil, the son of Qainan, the son of Yanish, the son
> of Shith, the son of Adam.[30]

What is more, the Prophet's significance for the salvation of the world must be demonstrated from the outset for Muhammad, as it was with Jesus – through the annunciation of his life on earth, at his birth and during his early childhood. This parallel is difficult to swallow for orthodox Muslims who keep strictly to the Qur'an. The Swedish religious historian Tor Andræ, to whom Western scholarship of Islam owes the first in-depth study of *Die Person Muhammads in Lehre und Glauben seiner Gemeinde* (*Muhammad in the Teachings and Faith of His Community* – 1918) pointed out that ideas about the wonderful origins of the figure of the Prophet were 'particularly noteworthy' in Islam. Why? 'It was clear from the start – the Qur'an had explicitly stressed this point – that the Prophet had only been chosen through an inexplicable act of

God's mercy. His selection was by no means ordained by a miraculous otherworldly intervention, and it had not altered the messenger's human characteristics. The one great miracle, which is merely confirmed by all the other signs, is the sending of the divine Book. This occurred on the holy night of *al-Qadr*, when the wonderful power weaves its glittering veil, every time the heavens bend down to the earth.'[31]

In fact, from beginning to end, the Qur'an never leaves the reader in any doubt that Muhammad is merely a man. Sura 7, from the late Meccan period, declares once and for all: 'their companion [...] is giving clear warning' (Sura 7:184). The theological reasoning for this self-definition is to be found in the Qur'an's typical annunciation of divine omnipotence: God alone determines men's fortunes, and He therefore also knows when the crucial moment in world history – Judgment Day – will dawn. It would therefore be absolutely inappropriate to talk up Muhammad as a miracle-worker, either at his birth or during his prophetic career. In his book *Der Koran. Einführung – Texte – Erläuterungen* (*The Qur'an. Introduction – Texts – Explanations*, 1991), Tilman Nagel, a scholar of Islam at the University of Göttingen, accurately stated: 'Muhammad is just an ordinary man; the Qur'an points that out explicitly. He eats the same dishes as his fellow men, and he visits markets as they do. His fellow men cannot understand that his authority relies on God's word alone, which was revealed to him. No angel appears at the Prophet's side;

the God whose message he proclaimed has not even endowed him with any earthly goods, treasure or a constantly flowering garden. Yet Muhammad is convinced that his own actions are not so essential to the work that he is supposed to accomplish. Quite the opposite: if it is to endure, then a mortal must efface himself entirely behind the word of God.'[32]

This portrayal is significantly revised in subsequent Islamic texts. If we are to believe Ibn Ishaq, Muhammad's mother Amina heard a wondrous voice *during her pregnancy* telling her: 'You are pregnant with the lord of this people and when he is born say, "I put him in the care of the One from the evil of every envier", then call him Muhammad.'[33]

In addition, Muhammad's mother remembers after his birth that she saw a light come forth from her while she was pregnant 'by which she could see the castles of Busrah in Syria'. She had never had 'a pregnancy which was easier or lighter than this'. When he was born, her child 'put his hands on the ground, lifting his head towards the heavens'.

According to a different text, written by Ibn Abbas, Muhammad's cousin, who had made a name for himself in the early Islamic community as an exegete of the Qur'an (he died around 687 AD), the Prophet's very conception was accompanied by a number of miraculous signs. All the domestic animals belonging to Muhammad's tribe had spoken that night. It had been the beasts that had announced that Muhammad was 'imam of the world and the light of its inhabitants'. Ibn Abbas says that the thrones of kings around the world had crumbled the next morning. Wild beasts in the East had rushed to bring the good tidings to animals in the West. Even the creatures of the seas had rejoiced together.[34]

Furthermore, according to Ibn Abbas's account, Muhammad's mother experienced the following in her seventh month of pregnancy:

> When six months of my pregnancy had passed, someone came to me in a dream and said, 'Amina, you are pregnant with the best of men. When you have given birth to him, call him Muhammad, but keep it a secret.'
>
> Then there befell me what befalls women […] I heard a great crash and a mighty sound, and it struck me with terror – that was on a Monday. I saw [a vision] as if the wing of a white bird stroked my heart, and then all the alarm, panic and suffering that I had felt left me. […] My labour became intense. I heard the crashing becoming louder and more fearsome all the time. Suddenly I saw a piece of silk brocade stretched between the heavens and the earth, and a voice was saying 'Take him where no one can see him.' […] I saw a flock of birds that had come down without my noticing from whence they came, until they covered my chamber. Their beaks were made of emerald and

their wings of rubies. The veil was lifted from my sight and at that moment I saw the eastern and the western regions of the earth. I saw three banners raised, a banner in the east, a banner in the west and a banner on the top of the Ka'ba. The labour pains gripped me and I was in great distress. I felt as if I were leaning against the limbs of women; they became numerous, to the point where it was as if there were many hands in the house, but I did not see anything. I gave birth to Muhammad; when he came out of my belly I turned and looked at him, and lo and behold, I saw him prostrating himself, with his finger raised like one who was pleading and supplicating.[35]

Miraculous signs during and after the birth

We will need to examine all these passages, but for now let us merely confirm the details. There were miraculous signs at the conception and during Muhammad's mother's pregnancy, and there were also miraculous signs during and after the birth of the Prophet. In Ibn Ishaq's portrayal, Muhammad's mother entrusted the newborn baby to a nanny called Halima. About this nanny we hear:

- Halima suddenly has as much milk as the baby can drink in her dry breasts. Halima's husband recognises that she has been given 'a blessed person'.

- The female donkey on which Halima rides with the boy Muhammad runs so fast that nobody can keep up.
- Halima reports that one day two men in white robes seized Muhammad, threw him to the ground, opened his chest and shook his heart. His foster parents conclude from this that a genie had entered the boy, and that great things would come of him!

These events are confirmed further on in Ibn Ishaq's account, with an appeal to the Prophet himself. The Prophet apparently later said to some of his companions:

I am what Abraham, my father, prayed for and the good news of my brother Jesus. When my mother was pregnant with me she saw a light proceeding from her which showed her the castles of Syria. I was suckled among the Banu Sa'd bin Bakr, and while I was with a brother of mine behind our tent shepherding the lambs, two men in white raiment came to me with a gold basin full of snow. Then they seized me and opened my belly, extracted my heart and split it; then they extracted a black drop from it and threw it away; then they washed my heart and my belly with that snow until they had thoroughly cleaned them.[36]

Although Ibn Abbas's account diverges from the one above, it does point in the same direction:

> Then I saw a white cloud that had come from the sky come down until it covered him and he was concealed from my sight; I heard a voice call out, 'Take Muhammad around the east and the west of the world; take him into all the oceans, so that they will know his name, his description and his form, and they will know that in [the oceans] he is called "al-Mahdi" ("the Effacer") because there is no polytheism but that it will be effaced by him in his time.' Then [the cloud] revealed him again in the twinkling of an eye, and lo, he was clothed in a woollen robe that was whiter than milk, and underneath him was a piece of green silk. He was grasping three keys of brilliant white pearl, and a voice said, 'Muhammad has grasped the keys of victory, the keys of the wind and the keys of prophecy.'[37]

Muhammad – a historic event

What happened in these accounts to the figure of 'the companion [...] giving clear warning'? What happened to the man who, according to the Qur'an, encountered resistance, rejection and persecution, and was indeed declared pathological from the very first moment he appeared in public? The man who was confronted with criticism from

those around him that he was one of the insignificant and
the lowly (see Sura 43:31; 11:91), who himself admitted
that he had been an 'orphan' (Sura 93:6) and whom God
had 'found in need' (Sura 93:8). The Muslim tradition now
reports of this man:

- His very conception is an event that shakes the
  whole human and animal kingdom.
- There were already supernatural interventions
  ('white wing'), visionary experiences ('light', 'white
  raiment') and miraculous events ('a flock of birds
  had come down') during his mother's pregnancy.
- His very birth is a redemptive event. The happenings are accompanied in wondrous fashion by
  angelic figures. The Prophet himself has his chest
  purified and is thus uniquely selected by God.
- The new-born child immediately proves that he is
  God's chosen one ('with his finger raised like one
  who is pleading and supplicating').
- As a boy, Muhammad is treated to a miraculous
  cleansing ritual by two male figures.

How can any of this easily be reconciled with the image
of Muhammad in the Qur'an? The intention is clear:
this kind of legendary embellishment serves to portray
Muhammad as *the* 'imam of the world and light of its
people' and as 'the best of men'. The aim is also to interpret his coming into the world as a moment of salvation

that has an impact on the whole of history, with the Ka'ba as the centre of the world. It is therefore no accident that the place with the three banners (one in the east, one in the west and one on the top of the Ka'ba) has become an emblem of the Islamic world. Tor Andræ, whose 1918 study we have already encountered above, was therefore able to state in his still very readable book *Mohammed: The Man and His Faith* (1932):

> Concerning Mohammed's birth miraculous things are related, such as were told earlier concerning the births of Moses, Buddha, Alexander, Jesus, Mary, and many others. In the hour of his birth a brilliant light shone over the entire world from East to West. With miraculous clairvoyance Amina saw the palaces of Syria and the necks of the camels in Busrah. When Mohammed was born he fell to the ground, took a handful of earth, and gazed toward heaven. He was born clean and without a spot, as a lamb is born, circumcised, and with the navel-cord already cut.[38]

Muslim 'Christmas'

Annemarie Schimmel also showed in her book *And Muhammad is His Messenger* (1981), which draws on Tor Andræ's studies, how adoration of the Prophet became linked with the celebration of his particular birthday over the course of Muslim history from the Middle Ages onwards. Muhammad is traditionally said to have been born in Mecca on 'Monday, the 12th day of Rabi' al-Awwal in the year of the elephant', which is the year 570 by the Islamic calendar. However, the custom of staging elaborate ceremonies to celebrate Muhammad's birth appears to have first arisen during the Fatimid Caliphate (969–1071 AD), since the Fatimids regarded themselves as descendants of the Prophet through his daughter Fatima. This is roughly equivalent to the development of the Christian tradition, for, as we have heard, it was a good 300 years before a festival was introduced to mark Jesus' birth.

In the meantime, the Prophet's birthday, known as *Mawlid*, had developed into one of the three great holy days of the Islamic world, alongside the festival marking the end of Ramadan and *Eid-al-Adha*, which coincides with the *Haj*, the annual pilgrimage to Mecca. The Dutch scholar of Islam Hans Jansen correctly reminded us in his 2008 biography of Muhammad, though: 'But that wasn't always so. The Prophet's birthday has only been regarded as a major Islamic holiday since the Middle Ages. As late as 1300, the militant orthodox theologian Ibn Taimiyya thought that it was wrong to celebrate Mawlid for three reasons: (1) there was no consensus about the Prophet's birth date; (2) the Mawlid festival was derived from the Christian Christmas; and (3) early generations of Muslims did not habitually celebrate this holiday. Yet the Mawlid of the Prophet was celebrated, for example, around 12 April in 2006 and around 2 April in 2007.'[39]

Do such comparative conclusions facilitate dialogue? Only to a very limited extent. First and foremost, they could be misused to outdo or even trump the other religion. Christians and Muslims might be tempted to use the birth stories to back up their claim that Jesus or Muhammad was the greater redeemer. The birth stories can confirm the respective followers in their beliefs in the divine missions of their instigators. Conversely, however, comparisons between the two religions' histories can also bring humility and modesty. All religions follow similar structural developments: idealisation, stylisation and verification by means of alleged miracles. Seeing through these basic human 'interests' allows us to acknowledge the danger that our own religion might indulge in triumphant self-idealisation, which is what closes down the possibility of dialogue. It doesn't build bridges, it fosters isolationism, leaving no room for any other religion before God.

We take a very different path in this book, seeking not to play traditions off against one another but to make them the subject of a more enriching conversation. It is not about comparing Jesus and Muhammad. Rather, we trace the New Testament accounts within the Qur'an itself and show how the Qur'an has already had a 'dialogue' with the stories of Jesus' birth. Instead of weighing the messages of the Bible and the Qur'an against each other, we want to forge links between them. If undertaken in the correct spirit, identifying the presence of our own stories in the other's book, and the reception of the other's in our own, nurtures communication and dialogue. What we have in common emerges, without obscuring the things that distinguish us. So let us get to work.

PART THREE

The Birth of John the Baptist in the Qur'an

John and Jesus met and John said, 'Ask God's forgiveness for me, for you are better than me.' Jesus replied: 'You are better than me. I pronounced peace upon myself, whereas God pronounced peace upon you.' God recognised the merit of them both.

Ahmad ibn Hanbal († 855)[40]

John the son of Zachariah met Jesus the son of Mary, John smiling of face and welcoming while Jesus was frowning and gloomy. Jesus said to John, 'You smile as if you feel secure.' John said to Jesus, 'You frown as if you are in despair.' God revealed, 'What John does is dearer to Us.'

Abu Bakr ibn Abi al-Dunya († 894)[41]

Mary is the model independent woman. She senses at an early stage that she has a spiritual tie with the Creator and shapes this relationship in her own way. She does extraordinary things for her sex and her time.

Der Koran für Kinder und Erwachsene
(The Qur'an for Children and Adults)[42]

There is no need to go into the many historical questions here: the presence of Christianity in Arabia during the lifetime of Muhammad in the sixth and seventh centuries, split between Rome and Byzantium, split into several groups and churches, all branding one another heretics; the presence of Christian communities on the Arabian peninsula, apparently mainly in northern Yemen, whereas there were never any Christian communities in Mecca and Medina; the presence in the region of individual Christians, whom Muhammad met on his travels and who may have influenced his views on Christianity; the image of Christianity and Christians in the Qur'an, and the continuing Islamic dispute with Christianity down through history. All these issues have been adequately explored in a number of historical essays.[43] In the following section we shall confine ourselves to analysing the suras that describe the births of John the Baptist, Mary and Jesus.

1. The 'John' sura in Mecca: 19:2–15

Jesus (Isa in Arabic) appears in fifteen of the Qur'an's 114 suras. The first mention, chronologically speaking, occurs in Sura 19 from the middle Meccan period and, eye-catchingly, he already features in conjunction with John and Mary. The context is important.

The primary message of the Qur'an

While focusing on Sura 19, it is important to realise that it was preceded by 57 earlier suras from Mecca. This means that half of the Qur'an has already been 'annunciated', and the basic themes of the Prophet's message had therefore been introduced and revealed long before. The Prophet had also long since incorporated into his annunciation substantial amounts of material with which Jews and Christians were familiar from the Hebrew Bible and post-biblical accounts, including the stories of the Creation and the Last Judgment, and those of Noah and Moses as well as Abraham and Ishmael.

It is thus no coincidence that Sura 19 should feature such passages in the following order. Longer passages of narration and dialogue about the births of John and Jesus (Sura 19:2–33) precede verses about a dispute over the image of Jesus (19:34–40) that appear to have been inserted at a later date, then – in an abrupt change of subject that is typical of the Qur'an – there follows a passage about Abraham and his clash with his father over the right way to worship God (Sura 19:41–48) and a passing reference to Isaac and Jacob (19:49). Then, just as suddenly, come a few verses about Moses and his conversation with God on the mountain along with an allusion to his brother Aaron (19:51–53), followed by a further extremely succinct reference to prophets such as Ishmael and Idris (Sura 19:54–56) and other prophets 'from the seed of Adam' including Noah and others

(19:58). Sura 19 concludes with another longer passage typical of the Qur'an about the Final Judgment with two possible outcomes: the Gardens of Paradise ('Garden of Eden') for believers (Sura 19:60–65) and the Judgment of God for unbelievers (Sura 19:66–98), especially those who claim that God has 'offspring' (19:88), without any reference to the controversy around Christ in verses 34–40 of the same sura. That someone might 'attribute offspring' to 'the Lord of Mercy' is now portrayed as a 'terrible' thing, associated with images of looming apocalypse (19:88–91). Sura 19 ends with a reminder, in the form of a message of warning and judgment characteristic of the Meccan annunciation, which relates the prophetic self-confidence of the annunciator in impressive fashion:

93 There is no one in the heavens or earth who will not come to the Lord of Mercy as a servant.

94 He has counted them all: He has numbered them exactly

95 and they will each return to Him on the Day of Resurrection all alone.

96 But the Lord of Mercy will give love to those who believe and do righteous deeds.

97 We have made it easy, in your own language [Prophet], so that you may bring glad news to the righteous and warnings to a stubborn people.

98 How many generations We have destroyed before

them! Do you perceive a single one of them now,
or hear as much as a whisper?

(Sura 19:93–98)

We shall come on to how the thematic structure of Sura
19 develops in spite of its abrupt changes of subject. First,
however, we shall turn to the question of why it is only
now, in Sura 19 and therefore in the middle Meccan
period, that stories from the Christian tradition appear
in the Qur'an, i.e. the first citations of these traditions,
whereas accounts of Old Testament and Jewish origin
have long been part of the Qur'an's 'teaching material'.
Why is this? What was the real reason for the composition of Sura 19? Who might its first Meccan audience have
been at the time?

We still lack a satisfactory historical explanation for
this. The Muslim tradition has linked the emergence of
Sura 19 to part of the original Muslim community's exodus
to Ethiopia. This sura, which is titled 'Mary', was recited
to the local negus ('king') and he was so impressed by
the Muslims' acknowledgement of Mary and Jesus that
he granted them his hospitality. There may be no way
of verifying this story historically, but it is of profound
symbolic significance (there are further details in the epi-
logue to this book, 'The "Mary" sura and the example of
Ethiopia'). In strictly historical terms therefore, we must
accept that there is no adequate explanation of why the
Qur'an only now begins to engage with 'Christian' figures

such as John, Mary and Jesus, even though Old Testament Jewish accounts had long been part of the prophetic annunciation.

Here too, however, there is good reason to believe that at the latest by the time they were incorporated into the prophetic annunciation, the New Testament Christian accounts must have been as familiar to the audience in Mecca as the Old Testament Jewish references were. By expanding his 'teaching material' to include Christian accounts, Muhammad shows that he is incorporating a second major religious tradition for political reasons. Linking his message to Christian sacred history in this way increases its persuasiveness. In future, he will be able to refer not only to the Jewish tradition but also to Christian teachings, interpreting them so that they are compatible with his own prophetic message while also challenging his audience in Mecca. The Paderborn-based Catholic theologian Klaus von Stosch seems to support this observation. He emphasises the fact that in a context of quarrelling among Jewish and Christian groups (Suras 43:63 and 19:37) during the middle Meccan period, the Qur'an was an invitation to form 'a single monotheistic community, which is meant to accommodate Christians too and therefore includes and reformulates some very specific statements about Jesus and Mary as part of its own message'.[44]

There are two immediately noticeable features of the text itself. For one thing, the very first mention of John the

Baptist (*Yahya* in Arabic) and Jesus are strikingly associated with the respective stories of their miraculous births. This is no accident: a focus on the birth stories is part of the Qur'an's theological manifesto. We shall study the contents of this manifesto later. Second, like the New Testament (Matthew 1:1–2, 12; Luke 1:1–2:20) the Qur'an contains two accounts of the birth of Jesus, namely in Sura 3:37–49 (Medinan period) and in Sura 19:1–36 (middle Meccan period). Sura 19 is the older of the two, so it is logical that we should turn our attention to this passage first.

John's miraculous birth

Christian readers will note with interest that, in the Qur'an as in Luke's Gospel, the story of the birth of John the Baptist precedes that of the birth of Jesus. Strictly speaking, neither of them is a birth story, but rather a story of annunciation. That is because John does not personally appear as a character in the following passage. Unlike the New Testament, the Qur'an does not relate the story of his life. The entire focus is on the *conditions* for his birth, which is the essential reason why his father Zachariah comes to the fore. He becomes a reflection of the surprising events that are told:

2   This is an account of your Lord's grace towards His
    servant, Zachariah,

3   when he called to his Lord secretly, saying,

4   'Lord, my bones have weakened and my hair is
    ashen grey, but never, Lord, have I ever prayed to
    You in vain:

5   I fear [what] my kinsmen [will do] when I am gone,
    for my wife is barren, so grant me a successor – a
    gift from You –

6   to be my heir and the heir of the family of Jacob.
    Lord, make him well pleasing [to You].'

7   'Zachariah, We bring you good news of a son
    whose name will be John – We have chosen this
    name for no one before him.'

8   He said, 'Lord, how can I have a son when my wife
    is barren, and I am old and frail?'

9   He said, 'This is what your Lord has said: "It is easy
    for Me: I created you, though you were nothing
    before."'

10 He said, 'Give me a sign, Lord.' He said, 'Your sign
    is that you will not [be able to] speak to anyone for
    three full [days and] nights.'

11 He went out of the sanctuary to his people and
    signalled to them to praise God morning and
    evening.

12 [We said], 'John, hold on to the Scripture firmly.'
    While he was still a boy, We granted him wisdom,

13 tenderness from Us, and purity. He was devout,

14 kind to his parents, not domineering or rebellious.

15 Peace was on him the day he was born, the day he

died, and it will be on him the day he is raised to
life again.

(Sura 19:2–15)

Thus, like Luke's Gospel, the Qur'an puts the annunciation of the birth of John before the actual story of the
birth of Jesus; and the Qur'an, like the Evangelist, is,
here too, interested in God's surprising intervention in
the case of John.[45] When comparing sources we should,
however, note that the Qur'an does not record the subsequent details of the Christian John the Baptist's life, for
example his appearance as a preacher of repentance
(in Luke 3:1–8; Matt. 3:1–12; Mark 1:1–8), his baptism of
Jesus (Luke 3:21–22; Matt. 3:13–17; Mark 1:9–11) or his
imprisonment and death at the hands of King Herod (Luke
3:19–20; Matt. 6:17–29; Mark 14:1–12). This is not where
its interest lies. John is mentioned four times in the Qur'an
– three times in relation to his miraculous origins (along
with Suras 19 and 3, also in Sura 21:89–90), and his name
appears a fourth time simply as one in a formulaic list of
figures, as one of the 'righteous' (Sura 6:85).

Comparing John in Luke's Gospel and the Qur'an

A careful comparison of Sura 19:1–15 with Luke 1:5–25
also reveals noteworthy differences in the theological
profiles. Luke the Evangelist situates his story of John in
vivid detail and sets it in a precise historical context. His

father Zachariah is a priest at the temple in Jerusalem and belongs to the division of Abijah; John's mother is called Elizabeth and she is a daughter of Aaron. The angel Gabriel, 'who stands in the presence of God' (Luke 1:19), appears to Zachariah. This appearance occurs in a real place, Jerusalem, and, more precisely, in the temple. This embeds John the Baptist's coming from the very beginning in his – the Jewish – people's wait for the Messiah. Gabriel then announces to Zachariah that he will have a son, who will 'go before Him in the spirit and the power of Elijah' and 'turn many of the children of Israel to the Lord their God' (Luke 1:16–17). Accordingly, Luke lets this temple priest pronounce a hymn of praise (the 'Benedictus') praising the 'Lord God of Israel' because 'He has visited and redeemed His people' (Luke 1:68).

The Qur'an, on the other hand, explicitly removes all geographical and historical information. The sole actor it requires is Zachariah. Only he speaks, with the exception of one line of dialogue from God. No angel appears here. In the Qur'an, Zachariah communicates directly with God. Elizabeth is not mentioned by name, as she is in the Bible, but purely as an adjunct of her husband: 'my wife is barren'. The site of their encounter is mentioned only indirectly and in passing ('sanctuary', Sura 19:11). John himself is given no voice of his own, and so we learn nothing about his annunciation. He is spoken *about*, and what is said is full of praise: he was given a name granted to 'no one before him', 'wisdom' even as a boy, and 'purity'; he was 'devout', 'kind to his parents' and not 'domineering', and so the scene can logically end with a blessing from God (19:15).

The whole scene appears carefully crafted, as if diluted, abstracted, disembodied. That is the intention, for the Qur'an is not interested in Zachariah as a real-life historical figure of Judaism. Why should it be at the beginning of the seventh century in the Arabian peninsula when there are no Jews in Mecca? Instead, it is interested in Zachariah as a timeless archetype – as an archetypal God-fearing believer whose highly private prayer ('secretly') is heard by God. He prays for the birth of an heir to his office at the temple in spite of his great age and his wife's obvious infertility. The start of Sura 19 is therefore entirely focused on the request and worship of a man who has never prayed 'in vain'. This sura can, and should, therefore remind people of God's 'mercy' as a signal to all unbelievers in Mecca, and that is why it can omit all the other historical details that are so central to the New Testament account. The Qur'an's interest in Zachariah and John is different, and must be different if this story is to be at all clear to its audience in Mecca.

The striking thing, indeed, is that Zachariah in Luke's Gospel had obviously been presenting his wish to God in prayer for so long that he can barely believe that at his age it is finally being granted. 'Your prayer is heard' are the angel's first words to Zachariah (Luke 1:13). In Sura 19, on the other hand, Zachariah appears to have expressed his wish for the very first time, conscious of the fact that he has never prayed to God 'in vain'. In Luke, Zachariah remains steadfastly sceptical, even when the angel appears ('How shall I know this?', Luke 1:18) and for this profession of disbelief he is struck dumb, a punishment that will last for the full nine months until the birth of John (Luke 1:63–64). In Sura 19, on the other hand, he is only deprived of speech for three days, and this 'sign' is not a result of God's punishment but of his trust in God's might. The signal to the audience is clear: in the same way that God the Creator is able to give an old, infertile couple an heir ('It is easy for Me': Sura 19:9), the same God can also send a signal by rendering a person speechless for a while. This speechlessness in the Qur'an is not a sign of punishment but a sign from heaven, one of God's many powerful acts.

That is the crucial element here, and it explains why the Christian story of Zachariah and John has been given a new Muslim twist to suit a conflictive situation with the unbelievers in Mecca, who are doggedly opposed to the Prophet's key message that one should lead a responsible life before the face of God. Yet Sura 19:2–15 uses the 'case of John' as another vivid illustration of the sovereign power of God the Creator and also as a means of instilling trust in people that their private prayers to God will never be 'in vain'. The truly devout can place their full trust in God's mercy, even if they can obviously never predict God's response. That too is demonstrated by the 'case of John', for God does not answer Zachariah's request in the way the latter had obviously been expecting. His son John will not take over his office in the temple: he will become a prophet in his own right. This is yet another signal in religious politics: the Qur'an is not interested in continuing the Jewish temple cult. It does not consider putting a Benedictus into Zachariah's mouth. Why would it? Temple services in Jerusalem had long since ceased when Sura 19 was composed. The Romans destroyed the temple after capturing Jerusalem in 70 AD. By this time Jerusalem was under Christian Byzantine rule, which meant that, in these changed circumstances, the story of Zachariah was only of any interest if it were dehistoricised and rendered universal to make it intelligible also to its intended audience in Mecca.

Time for a change of scene.

2. The 'case of John' – a new interpretation in Medina: Sura 3

The Qur'an returns to the 'case of John' a second time in Sura 3 from the Medina period. The historical background was entirely different to the situation when Sura 19 was written, as we saw in Part One (Chapter 5). That is because we can date the core of Sura 3 (verses 3:59–64 would merit discussion in isolation) with a fair degree of accuracy, unlike Sura 19. There is an allusion to the Battle of Badr in the second year of the Hijra (Sura 3:123), which concluded with a Muslim victory in March 624 – an event of the utmost political and religious significance, including for future relations between Jews and Christians. That was because the Muslims felt that God supported them more than ever after their triumph at Badr. The text also refers to the Battle of Uhud, a mountain near Medina, fought a year later (Sura 3:166–168). This ended in a painful defeat for the Muslims and was regarded as a difficult test sent by God. Even the Prophet almost lost his life there (Sura 3:144–146), exacerbating the situation among his followers.

Conflict with the Jews in Medina

There was obviously tension and conflict among Muslims by this time, with people making sham conversions to Islam. As a result, exhortations for the community to stick together grow louder and more passionate: 'Obey God and the Messenger!' (Sura 3:32). In his commentary on the Qur'an, Adel Theodor Khoury highlights the most important aspect of this situation: 'The instability of the community and the fickleness of the hypocrites [among Muhammad's followers], which made them an internal threat, along with the outbreak of hostilities between Muslims and Jews in Medina, form the backdrop to some passages in the sura. There is repeated criticism of the hypocrites and the opposing Jews, as well as words of encouragement for believers about God's intervention and promises of rewards in the afterlife.'[46]

Disputes with the Jewish tribes and their learned representatives were indeed intensifying. It is in this context that we should situate the revisiting of the annunciation of the birth of John and the revisiting of the story of Mary and Jesus, as we shall see later. It is clear that it was high time for a re-interpretation of Sura 19, and it is no coincidence that the relevant passage starts with a reference to Jewish figures: 'God chose Adam, Noah, Abraham's family, and the family of Imran, over all other people, in one line of descent – God hears and knows all' (Sura 3:33–34).

Comparing the 'John' suras

From verse 38 onwards, the sura describes the annunciation of the birth of John, although once again it is Zachariah who is in the foreground:

38 There and then Zachariah prayed to his Lord, saying, 'Lord, from Your grace grant me virtuous offspring: You hear every prayer.'
39 The angels called out to him, while he stood praying in the sanctuary, 'God gives you news of John, confirming a Word from God. He will be noble and chaste, a prophet, one of the righteous.'
40 He said, 'My Lord, how can I have a son when I am so old and my wife is barren?' [An angel] said, 'It will be so: God does whatever He will.'

41 He said, 'My Lord, give me a sign.' 'Your sign,'
   [the angel] said, 'is that you will not communicate
   with anyone for three days, except by gestures.
   Remember your Lord often; celebrate His glory in
   the evening and at dawn.'

(Sura 3:38–41)

So what do we see when we carry out an intertextual
comparison with Sura 19?

1. It is striking that the annunciation scene seems
   on the one hand to have been truncated and on
   the other expanded. All the psychological details
   have now been 'left out': the references to the age
   of the parents and their fear of dying without children or heirs. What has been added is a speech
   by angels (Sura 3:39), which serves to distance the
   answer to Zachariah's prayer through creatures
   that are placed *between* God and the beseecher.
   Then God speaks again.

2. It is also noteworthy that John is given other titles
   in Sura 3. Sura 19 had already mentioned that
   John's name is without precedent, and there is
   a similar statement in Luke's Gospel (compare
   Sura 19:7 and Luke 1:61). However, the fact that
   the Qur'an now calls John 'noble and chaste, a
   prophet' (Sura 3:39) demonstrates how John has
   been elevated to the foremost rank.

3. In addition, it is remarkable that the Qur'an's mention of John being chaste casts us back to a basic trait of John the Baptist in the New Testament – John as an ascetic man crying in the wilderness (Matt. 3:3–4; Luke 3:2–4). But whereas in the New Testament John goes out into the wilderness to prepare the 'way of the Lord' by appealing to people to repent and convert, in the Qur'an John is himself a sign from God. To be more precise, the New Testament John must recognise during Jesus' baptism that there is divine proof that He is the ultimate sign from God ('This is My beloved Son', Matt. 3:17), whereas John in the Qur'an is himself a sign of God's might and power. In the Qur'an, John is a prophetic figure from ancient Judaism, who is 'muslimised' as a prophet so that he may be held up as a critical reflection of the behaviour of the contemporary Jewish community in Medina.

3. Comparing John in the New Testament and the Qur'an

We can therefore conclude three things about the image of John in Suras 19 and 3.

Not a 'forerunner' but a parallel figure to Jesus

Whereas the Evangelists use John as a figure of contrast with Jesus, as a mere harbinger who can then be outdone by Jesus to impressive effect, the Qur'an uses John as a parallel figure, in whom God has already accomplished a deed that he then repeats with the birth of Jesus. That is why the Qur'an, unlike the New Testament, shows no interest in John's background or subsequent fate. In Luke's Gospel, the stories of John the Baptist and Jesus were closely entwined – for Jesus' aggrandisement. It is no coincidence that after the conception (Luke 1:26–39) Mary, now pregnant, goes to see the pregnant Elizabeth, who is then given the task of confirming their order in 'salvation historical' terms: 'Blessed are you among women, and blessed is the fruit of your womb! But why is this granted to me, that the mother of my Lord should come to me?' (Luke 1:43). In the Qur'an, these two stories are unconnected, running in parallel, and the recurring motif of annunciation and birth is the only structural link between them. What is more, Luke describes a meeting between John and Jesus. Jesus allows himself to be baptised by John (Luke 3:21–22), but Luke leaves no doubt about John's subservience: 'One mightier than I is coming, whose sandal strap I am not worthy to loose. He will baptise you with the Holy Spirit and fire' (Luke 3:16). The John of the Qur'an, on the other hand, does not proclaim the superiority of Jesus as the 'Son of God' as the New Testament does (Luke 3:22, Matt. 3:17 and Mark

1:9–11, respectively), but demonstrates in its own fashion the superiority of God over what seems impossible for a human. The Christologically based 'history of salvation' (the New Testament) is systematically replaced by a theocentric history. The story of John, set long ago in the mists of time, is thus a means of highlighting the Prophet's contemporaneous standoff with the unfaithful in Mecca (Sura 19) and later with the Jews in Medina (Sura 3). The story of John should be read as an updating.

A demonstration of the power of the Creator

Whereas the New Testament needs John as a contrasting figure to Jesus (so that he may later surpass him), the story of John in the Qur'an is a further illustration of the power of God the Creator, who is capable of generating new life from the barren and the necrotic at will. What we should note here is that Luke the Evangelist has an angel announce the birth of John the Baptist, but he is 'conceived' not by the Holy Spirit but by Zachariah, who has miraculously regained his fertility (Luke 1:23–24). On the other hand, the Qur'an entertains no doubts that John is just as much a creature of God as Zachariah is ('I created you, though you were nothing before' (Sura 19:9) and is special, as Jesus will be later: they are created by the spirit despite their parents' previous physical incapacity. In short, the story of John in the Qur'an must be understood in theocentric terms to urge its addressees to have faith in God's leadership. This motif is further emphasised shortly afterwards in the Qur'an in the form of two verses about Zachariah and John, based on Sura 19: 'Remember Zachariah, when he cried to his Lord, "My Lord, do not leave me childless, though You are the best of heirs." We answered him – we gave him John, and cured his wife of barrenness – they were always keen to do good deeds. They called upon Us out of longing and awe, and humbled themselves before Us' (21:89–90).

This exclusive focus on a happy birth story in the case of John follows a material logic, since the drama of the parent-child relationship plays a special role in a birth story. The Qur'an uses this to drive home its point in Sura 19. If we examine the structure of Sura 19 closely again, it becomes clear that the story of John was simply a prelude to two more parent-and-child stories in the same sura: the one of Mary and Jesus, and that of Abraham and his father. These 'individual stories' in Sura 19 are therefore 'far from simply strung together', to cite Angelika Neuwirth; they are 'closely bound together by common motifs such as the thrice-mentioned parent-child relationship – which are negatively reflected once more in the polemic against God's paternity – or common patterns of behaviour such as the recurring instances of protagonists speaking quietly or secretly, or else falling silent'.[47]

All of these parent-and-child stories in Sura 19 have a theocentric and creation-theological goal. They are supposed to demonstrate to the primary audience that the

God announced by Muhammad had long ago shown the will and the power to breach natural, biological ties, laying down a marker of his creativity. An old married couple, Zachariah and his wife, are granted a son against all the odds of nature. Immediately afterwards, unmarried Mary falls pregnant without the intervention of a man and gives birth to a child. Lastly, Abraham contravenes tradition and the biological hierarchy to confront his father, who is still an 'idolater'. So whereas the indignant rejection of Jesus' status as the son of God disproves His 'paternity' (19:35 and 19:88), God's creative power is nonetheless presented in vivid terms. What story could be better suited to this end than a birth story? Both illustrative and dramatic, it can demonstrate the unconditional power of God the Creator. Why? Because birth stories capture the instant in which God creates life from nothing, proving himself the supreme creator. In a nutshell, we are to read the story of John as a theocentric account of creation theology. This objective is expressed in both suras in the short sentences: 'This is what your Lord has said: "It is easy for Me: I created you, though you were nothing before"' (Sura 19:9), or even more concisely: 'It will be so: God does whatever He will' (Sura 3:40).

PART FOUR

Mary, God's Chosen One

Let us return once more to Sura 19. We have not discussed Mary so far, but now she comes to the forefront
and with her, her son. It has been correctly observed in
this regard that in Jesus' first appearance in the Qur'an he
does not figure 'independently, but as a secondary character in a story about his mother, and he subsequently
remains closely tied to her'.[48]

1. Mary as the mother of Jesus: Sura 19

This is true, for the drama of another surprising birth is
above all Mary's drama. We shall first reproduce the text
in its entirety before attempting to analyse it in detail. The
passage about John in Sura 19 is immediately followed by
this command:

16 Mention in the *kitab* the story of Mary. She
    withdrew from her family to a place **to the east**
17 and secluded herself away; We sent Our Spirit to
    appear before her in the form of a perfected man.
18 She said, 'I seek the Lord of Mercy's protection

against you: if you have any fear of Him [do not approach]!'

19 but he said, 'I am but a Messenger from your Lord, [come] to announce to you the gift of a pure son.'

20 She said, 'How can I have a son when no man has touched me? I have not been unchaste,'

21 and he said, 'This is what your Lord said: "It is easy for Me – We shall make him a sign to all people, a blessing from Us."'

22 And so it was ordained: she conceived him. She withdrew to a **distant place**

23 and, when the pains of childbirth drove her to [cling to] the trunk of a palm tree, she exclaimed, 'I wish I had been dead and forgotten long before all this!'

24 but a voice cried to her from below, 'Do not worry: your Lord has provided a stream at your feet

25 and, if you shake the trunk of the palm tree towards you, it will deliver fresh ripe dates for you,

26 so eat, drink, be glad, and say to anyone you may see: "I have vowed to the Lord of Mercy to abstain from conversation, and I will not talk to anyone today."'

27 She went back **to her people** carrying the child, and they said, 'Mary! You have done something terrible!

28 Sister of Aaron! Your father was not an evil man; your mother was not unchaste!'

29 She pointed at him.

(Sura 19:16–29)

We shall commence our analysis with some observations about the text's style and structure.

The spirit of God appears to Mary

The first key story about Mary in the Qur'an begins, like those of Zachariah and John, without any transition and without any biographical links that might suggest how central it is to salvation history. Verse 15 concluded the episode on John with a blessing, but verse 16 immediately draws our attention to a new character: 'Mention the story of Mary', with an additional comment: 'in the scripture' (*kitab* in Arabic). What is this supposed to mean? Who is to 'mention Mary' in an existing or future 'scripture' (*kitab* in Sura 19:16 has sometimes been translated as 'book')? It is not easy to come to a definitive interpretation of this. It could mean either an existing scripture, or one that is to be written now or in the future, as the imperative form of the sentence suggests that the speaker is urging the Prophet to commemorate Mary in writing. Sura 19:2 therefore probably contains an allusion to the future Qur'an.

What is also noteworthy is that three geographical indications structure this first key Qur'anic text about Mary.

- The encounter with and conception by the spirit take place in 'the east' (Sura 19:16–21);
- The birth of Jesus takes place in a separate 'distant place' (Sura 19:22–26);
- Mary returns to her people in a third place (Sura 19:27–29).

Comparing the birth stories in Luke and the Qur'an

We shall first try to gain a better understanding of the first half of this passage.

16 Mention in the Quran the story of Mary. She withdrew from her family to a place **to the east**

17 and secluded herself away; We sent Our Spirit to appear before her in the form of a perfected man.

18 She said, 'I seek the Lord of Mercy's protection against you: if you have any fear of Him [do not approach]!'

19 but he said, 'I am but a Messenger from your Lord, [come] to announce to you the gift of a pure son.'

20 She said, 'How can I have a son when no man has touched me? I have not been unchaste,'

21 and he said, 'This is what your Lord said: "It is easy for Me – We shall make him a sign to all people, a blessing from Us."' And so it was ordained.

(Sura 19:16–21)

Any experienced Christian reader encountering this text will immediately draw parallels with the New Testament accounts, namely the Nativity as told by Luke. The concordance is striking. Luke the Evangelist includes a message from God to Mary, delivered by the angel Gabriel. In Sura 19, this message is spoken by the spirit of God. Luke, too, reported Mary's fearful reaction: she is 'troubled' by the angel's appearance and requires reassurance: 'Do not be afraid …' (Luke 1:29–30). In Sura 19, Mary, obviously intimidated by the sudden apparition, seeks the protection of the 'Lord of Mercy' (Sura 19:18): 'Depart if you are in fear of God' is how Rudi Paret has paraphrased this passage to make it clearer. Luke also recorded the young woman's doubt: 'How can this be, since I do not know a man?' (Luke 1:34). The corresponding section of Sura 19 runs: 'How can I have a son when no man has touched me? I have not been unchaste' (Sura 19:20). Luke had already conveyed a predication of the child to come: 'Son of the Highest' (Luke 1:32–35). In Sura 19, this reads: 'a sign to all people', a 'blessing from God' (Sura 19:21).

At the same time, there are crucial and unmistakable differences. Unlike the Evangelist, Sura 19 conspicuously emphasises the visionary character of this spiritual encounter. The spirit of God presents itself to Mary 'in the form of' a perfected man (Sura 19:17). Why? Because this can 'counter the thought from the very outset that Mary has conceived by this "man" – some see him as the equivalent of the angel Gabriel. The text itself only gives one comparison: the "spirit" is not a man incarnate, and Mary only perceives it with her senses'.[49] Furthermore, in literary terms this scene of annunciation in the Qur'an is more like a fine sketch than a fully fledged scene. Here too, it is obviously sufficient to provide abbreviations, allusions and the sparsest detail. All of a sudden Mary is there, without further introduction, preparation or context, nothing but an address to readers and listeners typical of the Qur'an: 'Mention ...' In accordance with the Qur'an's general style, the text not only seeks to cite the past but also to bring it up to date. It wishes to remind its audience, raise their awareness and, in doing so, raise the implications for the present. That is why the Qur'an confines itself to as little detail as possible in this scene. There is no interest here in the precise historical background that was so vital in Luke's story. We hear no mention of Rome, Bethlehem, Jerusalem or Nazareth. None of this is necessary for the Qur'an to make its point. It tells a new version of the Mary and Jesus story for its own purposes. But what are they?

Mary's withdrawal – making herself available for God

Mary withdrew to a 'place to the east' (Sura 19:16). No further detail is provided about this place, and it doesn't need to be named, even though Muslim interpretations in classical commentaries or prophetic legends tend to see it either as a place to the east of the temple in Jerusalem or as an allusion to the 'rising sun' in the east.[50] This is idle speculation, because in this case it is clearly not a question of identifying and fixing a location, but first and foremost about the 'withdrawal' itself – a movement of self-retraction, as it were. This is firstly a socially motivated withdrawal by Mary 'from her people', whose negative reaction ('unchaste') is suggested in the third part of the text (Sura 19:28). Secondly, it is for theological and symbolic reasons, something that is further underscored by the spatial details in the next verse ('secluded herself away': Sura 19:17). This means that she hid, withdrew and shielded herself from her usual surroundings. Retreating spatially means retreating into her body. In narrative terms, both of these aspects denote a deliberate disembodiment of the world described here, which becomes almost transparent through its lack of real-life detail.

This is her dramatic preparation for an encounter with God, here in the form of the spirit of God. When Mary has withdrawn from her normal social environment, and the world has become as transparent as a flimsy curtain – then she is ready for the encounter with God. 'The repeated mentions of withdrawal stress on the one hand Mary's total receptiveness and, on the other hand, her total dependency on God. Only thus, away from the world of men, away from all human possibilities – for instance, participation in conception – can she meet the angel, hear the promise, conceive Jesus as a virgin and then bring him into the world.'[51]

The dialogue between the angel and Mary is pared down to the essentials, with a conspicuous stylistic blend of real-life detail and majestic language. Fear on Mary's part, and pacification of that fear by the divine messenger; divine annunciation of the birth, and doubt in the mind of the woman Mary; annunciation of a supreme act of creation, and fear of being branded a harlot. For the second time in quick succession in Sura 19 comes the same response to human doubts, verbatim: 'This is what your Lord said: "It is easy for Me"' (Suras 19:9 and 19:21). This theocentric motif ties the story of Jesus to that of John.

We can conclude that:

1. In narrative terms, the first section of the first 'Mary' sura in the Qur'an is driven by two withdrawals by Mary – two seclusions that will make her completely receptive to God's spirit. This reconquered space and re-conquered body are meant as objective correlates for the openness of the world and humans for an encounter with the divine.

2. In theological terms, the first section is driven by the relevant person's trust in the power of God the Creator. This is no different from the Zachariah episode. Just as God has the power to call Zachariah and John into being, so he has the same power regarding Mary and her son. The latter is

conceived through God's will and exists solely
due to the power of God's word. It is no accident
that the first section concludes with the apodic-
tic and incontestable formulation: 'It is ordained'
(Sura 19:21).

3. This has significant implications for Mary's representation in the Qur'an. The Qur'an is not
interested in the aspects prioritised by Luke the
Evangelist. Luke stressed Mary's active participation, which is why, after some initial doubt, he
makes her agree to the divine annunciation: 'Let it
be to me, according to your word', which gave rise
to the 'Fiat' ('Let it be') that plays such a important role in later Mariology. Furthermore, shortly
afterwards Luke puts the words of a revolutionary anthem in Mary's mouth (the since-famous
'Magnificat'): 'He has put down the mighty from
their thrones, and exalted the lowly / He has filled
the hungry with good things / and the rich He
has sent away empty' (Luke 1: 52–53) and he lets
Mary store all the happenings around her son 'in
her heart' (Luke 2:51). In Sura 19, however, Mary
is a more passive figure, stylised into an absolutely devout individual who is the subject of a
divine miracle. She utters no 'Fiat' or 'Magnificat',
and there must be a plausible explanation for this.

4. The representation of Mary in Sura 19 resembles
less her portrayal in Luke's Gospel than the one

in the non-canonical Protevangelium of James, a
Christian scripture from the mid-second century.[52]
This text is regarded as having been 'extremely
influential in late Antiquity and strongly defined
the image of Mary in the Western ecclesiastical
tradition: her identity as the daughter of Joachim
and Anna, two saints of the Church'.[53] In this
earlier text, Mary is indeed the daughter of a
pious couple, Anna and Joachim. The couple is
initially childless before receiving a visit from an
angel, who announces the birth of a child, which
its mother, Anna, then immediately offers to God
as His servant in the temple. Accordingly, Mary is
brought to the temple aged only three and stays
there, entirely cut off from society, until the age
of twelve, where she was 'as a dove that is nur-
tured, and she received food from the hand of an
angel'.[54] There is no unequivocal historical evidence for this text's impact on the Qur'an. What
is certain is that the representation of Mary in the
Qur'an strongly resembles that found in Christian
scripture, since the focus of Sura 19:16–21 is not
on the salvatory significance of the birth of Jesus
as the start of a story of messianic liberation for the
people of Israel and the Gentiles (as expressed in
the 'Magnificat'), but exclusively on God's special
sign to a young woman who conceives without
a man. Mary is therefore a sign of God's creative

power and mercy, and at the same time a signal to all humankind, who should put their faith in this power over life and death.

Spiritual, rather than sexual, conception

Similar things can be said about the second half of the text. Let us take another look at it.

22 And so it was ordained: she conceived him. She withdrew to a **distant place**

23 and, when the pains of childbirth drove her to [cling to] the trunk of a palm tree, she exclaimed, 'I wish I had been dead and forgotten long before all this!'

24 but a voice cried to her from below, 'Do not worry: your Lord has provided a stream at your feet

25 and, if you shake the trunk of the palm tree towards you, it will deliver fresh ripe dates for you,

26 so eat, drink, be glad, and say to anyone you may see: "I have vowed to the Lord of Mercy to abstain from conversation, and I will not talk to anyone today."'

27 She went back **to her people** carrying the child, and they said, 'Mary! You have done something terrible!

28 Sister of Aaron! Your father was not an evil man; your mother was not unchaste!'

29 She pointed at him.

(Sura 19:22–29)

A few brief remarks to facilitate our understanding: the striking thing is that the conception process is omitted from the narrative. We hear that she is pregnant, but nothing else. Like Luke 1:35, Sura 19:22 is devoid of any sexual references. Apparently, it should not recall any mythological scenes of procreation between gods and humans. The silence between Sura 19:21 and 19:22 upholds the respect that humans owe to the divine. Later suras in the Qur'an (as in the New Testament) provide minimal explanation: Jesus is conceived by Mary with the aid of the spirit of God. The corresponding passages in the New Testament and the Qur'an are strikingly similar:

> The Holy Spirit will come upon you, and the power of the Highest will overshadow you (Luke 1:35).

> We breathed into her from Our Spirit and made her and her son a sign for all people (Sura 21:91; also: Sura 66:12; see also: Sura 4:171).

What is remarkable in Sura 19 is that the onset of Mary's pregnancy (Sura 19:22) is mentioned almost simultaneously with the 'pains of childbirth' (Sura 19:23) – without any transition, and without any further information. Typical of the Qur'an. All we discover is that Mary is now in a 'distant place'. This bold 'leap' in the narrative has caused Muslim exegetes to speculate on the length of Mary's pregnancy. The corresponding passage in the *Stories of the Prophets* is worth studying, as it shows the exceptional status that Mary enjoyed among Muslims from an early stage. This is underlined by the fact that people wonder about the length of her pregnancy (since it might potentially differ from that of a 'normal' pregnancy):

> Opinions differ among scholars about the length of Mary's pregnancy and the time at which she gave birth to Jesus. Some say that her pregnancy lasted nine months, as for other women. Some say eight months. That was another sign, for no eight-month-old child has lived, save Jesus. Others say six months. Others, three years. Others still say a single hour. Ibn Abbas says it means nothing other than that she conceived and gave birth immediately. There was one hour only between the conception, the birth and the moment when she withdrew, for God does not tell of any separation between the two events. He says, 'She conceived him; she withdrew to a distant place' (Sura 19:22), meaning a place that was far from her people. Muqatil says that Jesus' mother was pregnant with him for an hour, he was formed (in her womb) for an hour, and he was born at a time when the sun was ending its day. She was twenty years old. She had had two periods before she conceived Jesus.[55]

Let us set such gynaecological-theological speculation aside and concentrate on the literal meaning of the text.

Palm-tree and stream: Mary in Egypt?

Once she is pregnant, the Qur'anic Mary in Sura 19 withdraws one more time. The aforementioned 'distant place' conjures up images of a desert oasis, and this is confirmed by the other details of the location: 'stream [...] trunk of the palm tree [...] fresh ripe dates.' The secondary literature has drawn attention to parallels between this section of Sura 19 and pagan and non-canonical Christian accounts.[56] Christian parallels can be found in the Gospel of Pseudo-Matthew, a Christian book of veneration of Mary as the queen of virgins. It describes this event in relation to the flight of the 'Holy Family' into Egypt, but was written in the post-Qur'anic period (!), in the eighth or ninth century.[57] Nevertheless, we will quote in full this text, which had a considerable influence on Christian iconography and the later Muslim tradition, because it will allow us to highlight the nature of the content of Sura 19:24–26 even more clearly:

Now on the third day of their journey, as they went on, it happened that blessed Mary was wearied by too great heat of the sun in the desert, and seeing a palm tree, she said to Joseph, 'I should like to rest a little in the shade of this tree.' And Joseph led her quickly to the palm and let her dismount from her animal. And when blessed Mary had sat down, she looked up at the top of the palm tree and saw that it was full of fruits, and said to Joseph, 'I wish someone would fetch some of these fruits of the palm tree.' And Joseph said to her, 'I wonder that you say this; for you see how high this palm tree is, and I wonder that you even think about eating of the fruits of the palm. I think rather of the lack of water, which already fails us in the skins, and we have nothing with which we can refresh ourselves and the animals.'

Then the child Jesus, who was sitting with a happy countenance in his mother's lap, said to the palm, 'Bend down your branches, O tree, and refresh my mother with your fruit.' And immediately at this command the palm bent its head down to the feet of blessed Mary, and they gathered from it fruits with which they all refreshed themselves. But after they had gathered all its fruits, it remained bent down and waited to raise itself again at the command of him at whose command it had bent down. Then Jesus said to it, 'Raise yourself, O palm, and be strong and join my trees which are in the paradise of my Father. And open beneath your roots a vein of water which is hidden in the earth, and let the waters flow so that we may quench our thirst from it.' And immediately it raised itself, and there began to gush out by its root a fountain of water very clear, fresh, and completely bright. And when they saw the fountain of

> water, they rejoiced greatly, and quenched their thirst,
> and also all the beasts of burden and all the animals,
> and gave thanks to God.[58]

Although there are underlying patterns and ties between this and the earlier Qur'anic version of the 'palm and spring' miracle, it is nevertheless the differences that are most eye-catching. In the Qur'an, Mary's miraculous refreshment with dates and water is a divine wonder, which the new-born child merely points out: 'Your Lord has provided …' (19:24). In the Gospel of Pseudo-Matthew, Jesus brings about the miracle himself. He, a mere boy, orders the palm to stoop and raise itself; he orders the water to flow to slake their thirst. What is also noticeable is that the Qur'an is extremely restrained in its account of this event: it is not interested in embellishing the story as the later Christian account does. It is merely suggested to Mary that she shake the trunk (Sura 19:25); there is nothing miraculous about this. In the Christian source, the palm tree bends its branches spectacularly to the ground when the child orders it to do so, then raises itself again just as dramatically at his command.

Re-enacting the fate of Hagar

Whatever the relations and links between the two accounts in terms of motifs might be, in Sura 19:22–29 the Qur'an gives us the following signals:

1. The first thing that catches the eye is how skilfully the Qur'an employs contrast at this point in the text. On the one hand, the world is reduced to a handful of impressionistic details; on the other, there is a realistic depiction of the world, with the extremely vivid description of the astonishment of the people around Mary at an unmarried woman giving birth to a child, and their suspicions that she is a whore. Her desire to be partially or completely forgotten (Sura 19:23) is answered by God's kindness. Mary's desire to die is in contrast to the free-flowing spring water. Her bitter pains while giving birth contrast with the marvellous refreshment provided by sweet dates. The two times the newborn baby speaks respond to the adult Mary's vow of silence. Here, more than in the first part of the text, there is a deliberate literary contrast between realism and stylisation, between the lowliness of the everyday and the mightiness of the prophecy, between the specific details of a human story, and disembodiment that serves to make divine will clear.

2. In terms of structure, the scene of salvation through the flowing water has echoes of the salvation of Hagar depicted in the Book of Genesis (Gen. 21:14–19). One reason why this association is not so far-fetched is because Hagar plays a central role as the 'Mother of Islam' – not in the

Qur'an, but in the post-Qur'anic tradition.[59] It is inconceivable that the Prophet would not have been familiar with Hagar's story, for it is Ishmael, her son with Abraham, who embodies the Muslim connection with Abraham in the Qur'an (see Suras 2:127 and 3:54). According to both the Bible and the post-Qur'anic stories, Abraham and Sarah cast Hagar out into the wilderness with her thirteen-year-old son Ishmael, but God sends an angel to save them. Hagar finds a well of water, fills her flask and gives her son a life-saving drink (Gen. 21:19). So in both Genesis 21 and Sura 19, God miraculously saves the mother of the religion by providing a spring. It is clear that God's intervention in the fates of Mary and Hagar are to be equated. Hagar's fate also befalls Mary, so Mary can take her place in the salvation history of Islam too – as the archetypal original image of the mother of Islam.

3. There is a profound theological and symbolic significance in the Qur'an's choice of 'desert' or 'oasis' scenery rather than a stable (Luke 2:7) or a house (Matt. 2:11) as the setting for the birth of Jesus. The desert is a barren space, a place of emptiness, a place without any character of its own. This is why it is an ideal objective correlate to God's abundance, God's presence and God's coming into the world. At the same time, the palm

tree and its dates, along with the running water from the spring, are symbols of fertility, new life and the future. They stand for God's life-giving deeds. The choice of this setting, rather than a different one, underscores the creation-theological point of the entire Sura 19.

What are the ramifications for the image of Mary we encounter in Sura 19:16–33? Mary is portrayed here above all else as a saintly female figure, as the epitome of purity, who miraculously gives birth to an exceptional child. From the outset, Mary plays a significant role in the Qur'an as a woman who has been especially marked out by God. 'Mention in the Qur'an the story of Mary' (19:16): this is not intended merely as a slogan; it is a signal to the first unbelievers to hear it in Mecca, urging them to place their trust not only in God the Creator, but also in Mary. This makes Mary both noteworthy and notable. She is one of a list of people in human history who are impressed upon the audience of the Qur'an as a special sign of God the Creator. The title of Sura 19 contains the name 'Maryam'. A serious pronouncement is therefore attributed to the boy Jesus in Sura 19: to 'cherish' his mother. In one of the following suras, from the middle Meccan period, this leads to the fixed and formulaic words: 'We made the son of Mary and his mother a sign; We have them shelter on a peaceful hillside with flowing water' (Sura 23:50).

So who were the audience for such statements about

Mary? It cannot have been Christian groups. The texts do assume that the first to hear them are familiar with the importance of Zachariah, John, Mary and Jesus, but until 19:33 there is no mention of any controversies about Christology from which one might infer any conflicts with Christian denominations. By its portrayal of Mary and Jesus the Qur'an is actually establishing some distance between itself and 'pagans who obviously located Jesus in a divine pantheon similar to their own. Many Quranic utterings reflect Christian tradition without being marked as such, thus suggesting a high degree of familiarity with Jesus' teachings in the Meccan community. It is only in Medina, where dogmatically minded Christians entered the horizon of the community, that the debate was extended to include discussions about Christian positions and a more polemic attitude against particular Christian dogmas emerged'.[60]

2. Mary's birth and childhood: Sura 3

It is true that if we review the entire Qur'an, it becomes apparent that the commemoration of Mary is restricted to the few texts written in the second Meccan period. There is not a single word about Mary during the first and third periods. This only changes in Medina. Sura 3 not only features more statements about the births of John and Jesus, it also contains completely new declarations about Mary. For what reason?

Mary as a means of criticising the Jews

Here too, the reason is the confrontation with Medina's Jewish tribes and their learned representatives. We already saw this with John, whose story was also re-read and subjected to close critical examination in Medina (Part Three, Chapter 2). He had been unveiled politically as a prophet of both Judaism *and* Islam; the same now happens with Mary. Statements about her (Sura 19:16–33) are 'a rethinking of the until then unquestioned rank of the Israelites (Al Ibrahim) as the sole elects and transmitters of Scripture'.[61]

Mary's story does indeed re-emerge – in Sura 3 – in a Jewish context as a further sign from God that the Jews have already ignored once. This new emphasis is glaring, compared to Sura 19. Here, Mary is not described as the mother of Jesus. Instead, it is her own birth and childhood that are related, and the sura even provides a back story in which her own mother plays a central part, though Sura 19 does not mention her:

33 God chose Adam, Noah, Abraham's family, and the family of Imran, over all other people,

34 in one line of descent – God hears and knows all. Imran's wife said, 'Lord, I have dedicated what is growing in my womb entirely to You; so accept this from me. You are the One who hears and knows all,'

36 but when she gave birth, she said, 'My Lord! I have given birth to a girl' – God knew best what

she had given birth to: 'the male is not like the
female – I name her Mary and I commend her and
her offspring to Your protection from the rejected
Satan.'

37 Her Lord graciously accepted her and made her
grow in goodness, and entrusted her to the charge
of Zachariah. Whenever Zachariah went in to see
her in her sanctuary, he found her supplied with
provisions. He said, 'Mary, how is it you have these
provisions?' and she said, 'They are from God: God
provides limitlessly for whoever He will.'

(Sura 3:33–37)

Although the New Testament does not give the names
of Mary's mother or father, Christian tradition calls them
Anna and Joachim, as we know from the aforementioned
Protevangelium of James. Yet Sura 3 of the Qur'an is now
conscious of a father of Mary, 'Imran' (3:33), who would
therefore be the grandfather of Jesus (see also Sura 66:12).
This peculiar name probably refers to a biblical figure.
This is obviously meant to hark back to Amram, yet in the
Hebrew Bible he is the father of the brothers Moses and
Aaron and their sister Miriam (Num. 26:59). This creates
some problems of interpretation, since the Imran named
in the Qur'an is clearly the husband of Mary's mother
and hence her father. This verse was, and continues to
be, controversial and an occasional bone of contention
among exegetes.[62] The decisive point, nonetheless, is that

the Qur'an obviously wishes to stress the human ancestry of Mary and Jesus via this (at the very least indirect) mention of Mary having a father, and simultaneously highlights the historical stock from which Mary and Jesus are descended, i.e. the world of the Hebrew Bible. It is not by chance that 'the family of Imran' are linked to figures such as Adam and Noah and 'Abraham's family' in 3:33.

This lays the groundwork for the drama to come. As we hear in Sura 3:35, Imran's wife, the mother of Mary, dedicates her child to God before it is even born. The Qur'an explicitly picks up on the motif that we already know from the Protevangelium of James, and which was implied in Sura 19:16f. (see Chapter 2.1 in this section: *Mary's withdrawal – making herself available for God.*) Mary's mother offers her newborn child as a servant of God. It is not explained why she does this. Evidently only the act counts, underscoring that from the very beginning of her life Mary, the future mother of Jesus, is in the service of God. Her mother's profession of faith – 'You are the One who hears and knows all' (Sura 3:35) – rules out the fact that this dedication is a human initiative which takes God by surprise. It immediately reveals devotion to God. The new-born child is clearly intended to be the embodiment of piousness. The political calculus behind such a representation is obvious: to an even greater degree than in Sura 19, Mary is stylised as a woman resigned to God's will, i.e. as a model believer within Judaism, along with Adam, Noah and 'the family of Abraham', and as such she can be better employed against contemporary Jews with whom the Prophet is in dispute in Medina. Mary is therefore the ultimate Jewish archetype of a Muslim woman – a woman who is utterly devoted to God and, at the same time, shows up 'those who ignore God's revelations, who unjustifiably kill prophets, who kill those who command that justice is done' (Sura 3:21).

Early Christian parallels

Seen from this angle, we also understand why Sura 3 no longer mentions any problem with Mary's mother's pregnancy, as Sura 19 did, in complete contrast to the case of Zachariah, whose story comes up again in the same sura, as we have already heard (*The 'case of John' – a new interpretation in Medina: Sura 3*). The Protevangelium of James offers a further illustration of the scant regard the Qur'an pays to conflicts in this particular passage (conflicts between men or conflicts between man and God). This piece of scripture also tells us something about Mary's mother's background. Her mother Anna is infertile and bitterly laments her fate to God. In this she is like women such as Sarah in the Old Testament (Gen. 17:17) and Elizabeth in the New Testament (Luke 1:18). Anna beseeches God, quarrels with him and curses herself. First, this apocryphal infancy gospel describes the drama of a hitherto childless woman, but then it tells us:

Suddenly, an angel of the Lord stood in front of her, saying, 'Anna, Anna, the Lord God has heard your prayer. You will conceive and give birth and your child will be spoken of everywhere people live.'

And Anna said, 'As the Lord God lives, whether I give birth to either a male or a female child, I will bring it as an offering to the Lord my God and it will be a servant to him all the days of its life.'

[…] Then, Joachim came with his flocks. Anna was standing at the gate. When she saw Joachim coming with his flocks, Anna ran and wrapped herself around his neck, saying, 'Now I know that the Lord God has blessed me greatly. See, the widow is no longer a widow and the childless woman has conceived in her womb.'[63]

The description of the birth of Mary in Sura 3 is reported in a thoroughly undramatic fashion compared with the style of this text and of Sura 19. No indication here of a very old woman's infertility (as with Zachariah's wife in 19:8); no mention either of emotional turmoil between the man and woman. Quite the opposite: according to Sura 3 Mary's mother has had no trouble conceiving and before her child is even born, dedicates it to God, who 'hears' and 'knows' all: 'I have dedicated what is growing in my womb entirely to You; so accept this from me' (Sura 3:35).

It is only what follows that causes us to prick up our

ears. Why, after the birth, does she inform God in prayer that it is a 'girl', so that she must be corrected by God, 'who knows all': 'God knew best what she had given birth to: the male is not like the female' (Sura 3:36)? As if the introduction to this sura had not already announced that 'It is He who shapes you all in the womb as He pleases' (Sura 3:6). We perceive a hint of disappointment in the mother's voice here. Mary's mother had obviously hoped for a boy, and now she is wondering whether she will be able to keep her oath. Yet this surprising nuance in the text has little to do with cultural relativism – for instance, the fact that parents prized a boy more than a girl in the East in late Antiquity. That is not the message here.

The message is theocentric in nature. It is precisely because the reader is made aware of people's 'natural' and 'normal' reaction (disappointment at the birth of a girl) that the only possible conclusion is that God has shattered traditional conceptions about the sexes by granting Mary's mother a baby girl. He knows in advance that it will be a girl, for he has something special in store for her and affords her his special protection. It is no coincidence that her own mother is given a voice and allowed to speak directly to God in prayer (3:35–36). Sura 3 is therefore fundamentally about a 'female discourse' 'centred around female purity and the sacredness of pregnancy and childbirth'.[64] It is true that one detects a 'gender-informed subtext' in this sura. First, Mary is singled out as a positive female protagonist, and second, she is provided with a 'uniquely matrilineary genealogy' through the inclusion of her mother (a second female protagonist).[65] This is all done with the obvious aim (in the context of a dispute with contemporary Judaism!) of 'counterbalancing' the uniquely acknowledged lineage of Abraham. 'To embark on this theological venture, Mary and Jesus had to be stripped of the Christological implications, which from the perspective of the strictly aniconic monotheist mind set of the community must have seemed highly problematic.[66]

Mary's election by God

Sura 3 does at least give a glimpse of where Mary grows up: in the sanctuary. To this we may add: obviously in Jerusalem. This is where Sura 3:37 provides extra detail to the statement in 19:16–17, in line with the dedication to God announced earlier. The consecrated young woman lives in God's precinct, but the Qur'an gives very little detail. It is interested neither in the physical location nor in the relationship between Zachariah and Mary. Zachariah is allowed to look after the child, but no more. Realistic detail is vague, allowing the special sign related to this woman to come to the fore, *viz.* God's unique proximity to this special female, which is why there is a remark that Mary is provided for without any human intervention. She is provided for 'by God' in the understanding that 'God provides limitlessly for whoever He will' (Sura 3:37), meaning that he expects nothing in return. At this point in the Qur'an, Mary is the incarnation – which is possible in Judaism – of a life spent in trusting devotion to God, protected by God's care.

Zachariah makes another appearance in Sura 3:38–41 (see Ch. 1.4 in this part) before the story of Mary continues:

> 42 The angels said to Mary: 'Mary, God has chosen you and made you pure: He has truly chosen you above all women.
> 43 Mary, be devout to your Lord, prostrate yourself in worship, bow down with those who pray.'
> 44 This is an account of things beyond your knowledge that We reveal to you [Muhammad]: you were not present among them when they cast lots to see which of them should take charge of Mary, you were not present with them when they argued [about her].

(Sura 3:42–44)

Verses 42 and 43 pose no particular problems and can be grasped without any additional commentary, but we acquire a better understanding of the statement in Sura 3:44 ('You were not present among them when they cast lots …') by comparing it with another parallel text from the Protevangelium of James.[67] Although the latter does not inform us that Mary was placed in Zachariah's care, it does say that an angel appeared and told Zachariah, the high priest, to choose a husband for the 12-year-old

Mary, which he did by rods. All the widowers gather in the temple, among them an old man called Joseph. The priest takes the men's rods, enters the temple with them and waits for a sign from God. Joseph is chosen because a dove comes out of the rod and alights on his head.

Sura 3:44 alludes to this oracle of the rods to determine Mary's future. Whereas the Christian text cites Joseph by name as the chosen one, the name of Mary's future husband does not feature in the Qur'an – neither here nor anywhere else. The fact that Joseph is Mary's husband (and therefore the potential father of Jesus) is irrelevant to the Qur'an's message. On the other hand, there is a unique concentration of statements about Mary in this particular passage of the Qur'an. What is implicit in Sura 19:21–33 is made explicit – and almost political – here:

1. 'God has chosen you …' (Sura 3:42): Mary is one of God's chosen ones, which confirms Mary's special status 'above all women'. The additional comment that God has 'made her pure' is the condition for Mary being allowed to stay in the sanctuary, as the Qur'an has already noted. The fact that Mary has been 'made pure', i.e. free from sin, before she conceives Jesus is also important for the Christian tradition. The Qur'an is clearly alluding to this Mariological motif of the ancient Church.

2. 'Be devout to your Lord …' (Sura 3:43): Mary is the

ultimate embodiment of surrender to God's will. The three imperatives listed here – 'be devout', 'prostrate yourself' and 'bow down' – refer to the Muslim custom of prayer and its different postures. These two physical gestures, prostrating oneself and bowing, are recommended by a separate passage in the Qur'an: 'Believers, bow down, prostrate yourselves, worship your Lord, and do good so that you may succeed' (Sura 22:77). Mary sets an example of what the Qur'an demands all believers to do.

For all these reasons, i.e. because the Qur'an elevates Mary from birth to the status of a woman chosen by God, because she was protected and provided for by God as a child, made pure and free of sin, and because she is the absolute embodiment of devotion to God, it is appropriate to speak of theocentric Mariology in the Qur'an.

Spiritual conception and virgin birth

This theocentrically oriented Mariology is further underscored by the motif of creation by the spirit. Thus far, Sura 3 has differentiated itself from Sura 19 by mentioning Mary's birth and childhood. Now it adopts the same motif we saw in Sura 19: the annunciation of the birth of Jesus, the dialogue with the angel and God's act of creation:

45 The angels said, 'Mary, God gives you news of a
   Word from Him, whose name will be the Messiah,
   Jesus, son of Mary, who will

46 be held in honour in this world and the next,
   who will be one of those brought near to God.
   He will speak to people in his infancy and in his
   adulthood. He will be one of the righteous.'

47 She said, 'My Lord, how can I have a son when no
   man has touched me?' [The angel] said, 'This is how
   God creates what He will: when He has ordained
   something, He only says, "Be", and it is.'

(Sura 3:45–47)

We shall return later to the specific statements about
Jesus, but for now we shall concentrate on the representation of Mary. When we compare this passage with Sura
19, we notice the following:

1. Unlike in the Mecca version, here Mary does not
   have a vision but an 'audition'. The spirit of God
   does not appear to her 'in the form of a perfected
   man' as in Sura 19:17. Instead, she hears the voices
   of a number of (invisible) angels.

2. Mary's reaction appears to be even more stylised
   in Sura 3. There is no mention here of her double
   fear, as in Sura 19 – her fear of the sudden divine
   apparition, and her fear of being cursed for being
   'unchaste'. All that remains of Mary's elementary

human response in Sura 3 is the issue of the possibility of becoming pregnant without being touched by a 'man'.

3. The creative power of God is even more pronounced in Sura 3 than in Sura 19. Mary's agreement is not sought, and the woman is told even more clearly: 'This is how God creates what He will: when He has ordained something, He only says, "Be", and it is.'

The only woman mentioned by name in the Qur'an

Sura 66 from the Medina period offers another striking illustration of Mary's unique status in the Qur'an. It names four women – Noah's wife, Lot's wife, the Pharaoh's wife, and Mary. Noah's and Lot's wives 'betrayed' them and were handed over for Judgment, without further explanation. Pharaoh's wife and Mary are held up as examples:

11 God has also given examples of believers: Pharaoh's wife, who said, 'Lord, build me a house near You in the Garden. Save me from Pharaoh and his actions; save me from the evildoers,'

12 and Mary, daughter of Imran. She guarded her chastity, so We breathed into her from Our spirit. She accepted the truth of her Lord's words and Scriptures: she was truly devout.

(Sura 66:11–12)

It is worth pointing out something that Muslims often emphasise with no little pride in discussion with Christians, namely that the Qur'an refers to Noah's, Lot's and the Pharaoh's wives, but does not give their names; Mary is the only woman mentioned by name in the Qur'an. It is no wonder, then, that the Islamic religion affords her such significance.[68]

We can now summarise the evidence from the Qur'an. We shall do so in the words of two Catholic theologians, Ludwig Hagemann and Ernst Pulsfort, to whom we owe a short study called *Maria, die Mutter Jesu, in Bibel und Koran* (*Mary, the Mother of God in the Bible and the Qur'an*, 1992), which is still well worth reading today: 'Mary is also characterised in the Qur'an, along with her son, as a "sign for all men". God's actions can be read through her. She is seen as the archetype of a woman who is willing to believe and is held up as an example to believers. Just as the wife of the initially unbelieving Pharaoh professes her faith in prayer (Sura 66:11), just as the Queen of Sheba adopts the faith before the unbelieving people around her (Sura 27:23–33), so Mary is a believer among the unbelieving Israelites. This places Mary alongside Pharaoh's wife and the Queen of Sheba, and apart from the unbelieving wives of Noah and Lot (Sura 66:10–11), as an archetype and a prefiguring of the belief of Khadija, Muhammad's spouse, who is recorded as being the first woman convert to Islam. Islamic tradition regards Mary as one of the four best women that have ever lived, alongside Aisha, Khadija and Fatima, and she is considered the chief of all women in Paradise. Like Abraham (Sura 19:41), Idris (Sura 19:56) and Joseph, son of Jacob (Sura 12:46), Mary is given the title "siddiqah" in the Qur'an, which means "virtuous", "pious" and also "truthful". Because she accepted the truth of "her Lord's words and Scriptures", she is "truly devout" (Sura 66:12).'[69]

3. The cult of Mary in Islam

After all these explanations, the question now is what unites Muslims and Christians in their veneration of Mary, and what divides them?

Reflecting on Mary with Muslims

We saw that of the two New Testament Nativity stories, only the Gospel of Luke gives Mary her own role and her own theological profile. In summary, we can say: 'The shepherds and, in particular, Mary display the actions appropriate to God's deeds – not subservience and blind obedience, but active faith. In [Luke's] text, Mary is represented neither as a co-agent of salvation nor as an example of a meek woman, but as an archetypal believer, just as Abraham was. Her faith is doubly active: she understands, and she experiences what she believes in. Luke tells a story and quotes heavenly voices, staying true to his theological and literary manifesto. God acts through human situations, opening them up for faith through the testimonies of his witnesses.'[70]

There are remarkable similarities between Mary's representation in the Gospel of Luke and that in the Qur'an. *Neither in the New Testament nor in the Qur'an is Mary the agent of salvation, but nor is she simply a meek woman. She is the epitome of a believer. Christians and Muslims alike know that Mary was chosen by God. They know that Mary's purity is a symbol of her receptiveness to God, that Mary's meekness is a sign of her trust in God, and that Mary's faith is an expression of her devotion to God.*

At the same time, we should stress the elements that set Christians apart from Muslims. *Christians recognise the central role of Mary in the mission, message and fate of her son Jesus Christ. Mary's unique role in salvation history is due to the uniqueness of her son. Christian Mariology serves the centrality of Christ. The centrality of Mary in the redemptive message is alien to Muslims. Christians must be sensitive to the 'warnings' of their partners in dialogue when they bolt a Christ-centred interpretation onto theocentric Mariology. Christians do not view this addition as a replacement, but as a consolidation. What is true, in any case, is that any deification of Mary is incompatible with either how Mary is represented in the New Testament or with worship of Mary in the conciliary ecclesiastical tradition ('Mother of God').*

More recent exegetic and historical studies of Mary and Jesus by Muslims show various overlaps and differences. I refer the reader to studies by Muzaffer Andaç (2000), Nimetullah Akin (2002), Ahmed Ginaidi (2002)[71] and H. Ilker-Çinar (2007). Also, Annemarie Schimmel impressively demonstrated in her fascinating book *Jesus and Mary in Islamic Mysticism* (1999) 'how in the Islamic tradition Mary became a symbol for the human soul – the soul, which through God's mercy was miraculously able to give life to the highest form of wisdom'.[72] Schimmel was an early proponent of the opinion that Mary plays a major role in the 'overall tradition and religion' of Muslims. This could be judged from 'how pious Turks visit the alleged grave of Mary on the Bülbüldagi near Ephesus'.[73]

The legendary House of Mary at Ephesus

There is a chapel at around 500 metres in altitude on this hill near the ancient city of Ephesus (the present-day Turkish city of Selcuk). It is known as the house of Mary. The mother of Jesus supposedly spent the final years of her life here. The building's Turkish name is *Meryem ana evi* (literally, 'Mary Mother House'). The literal translation of Bülbüldagi is 'Nightingale Mountain'! According to tradition, John, Jesus' favourite disciple and the man who announced Christianity in Ephesus, brought Mary here after the Crucifixion, thereby respecting Jesus' final request to him: '"Behold your mother!" And from that hour that disciple took her to his own home' (John 19:27).

Curiously, we owe the fact that this place was called 'Mary's House' to an ostracised 19th-century nun, Anna Katharina Emmerick (1774–1824), who was beatified by Pope John Paul II not so long ago. Her 'visions' were taken down in writing by the author Clemens von Brentano (1778–1842). In 1833 he published the first part of his writings on Emmerick with the title *The Poor Life and Bitter Sufferings of Our Lord Jesus Christ, according to the Visions of the Blessed Anna Katherina Emmerick*. A second, posthumous book was 'added' by his brother Christian Brentano in 1852 and called *The Life of the Holy Virgin Mary*. This book was to have unintended consequences, for the precise details of the supposed last home and grave (!) of Mary supplied by this nun from Dülmen in Westphalia prompted French monks to set out for Ephesus in the late 19th century to look for it. They found a ruined house on 'Nightingale Mountain' that appeared to match Emmerick's descriptions.[74] They believed that they had discovered 'Mary's House'! This caused a major 'sensation', and by 1896 Pope Leo XIII had proclaimed the spot a pilgrimage site. His successor Pius X went so far as to grant pilgrims who reached the site full remission of their sins. Paul VI and John Paul II further promoted the site: the former undertook a pilgrimage there on 26 July 1967, the latter on 30 November 1979.

A place of pilgrimage for Christians and Muslims

The whole precinct around a chapel built on the ruins in the last century forms a uniquely peaceful spot. It also occupies a unique place in religious history, for not only Christians visit this site but Muslims too. Step inside the chapel today and turn right into Mary's 'sleeping chamber' and you will find some framed Mary-related verses from the Qur'an on the wall. Muslims too come here to pray.[75]

The chapel welcomes over a million Christian and Muslim pilgrims each year. They come here not least because they can find sacred water down a flight of steps under the house. People collect a little in the hope of a cure, and countless people have obviously enjoyed some release from their sufferings after visiting the spring. They have left tokens of their gratitude, as well as signs of their hope, their fears and their worries. Inside the precinct there is the impressive sight of a wall covered with thousands and thousands of slips of paper and pieces of fabric. Christian and Muslim pilgrims come together here in prayer. They ask Mary to present their cares to God, and show their gratitude when they have been released from their pains.

The Turkish religious scholar Ali Ihsan Yitik, who teaches at the Theological Faculty of the University of Izmir, described this phenomenon in an extremely interesting essay, *The Virgin Mary and Her House near Ephesus. A Comparative Mariological Study* (2000). He reminds us that statements in the Qur'an and other

Islamic texts describe Mary as a God-sent emissary, a prophetess indeed, or at the very least holy, virtuous, a witness and a god-fearing woman. Mary is 'in the opinion of many Turkish Muslims, a *noble* and *honest* woman and someone who intercedes with God'. To quote the Turkish scholar further: 'We find this conception predominantly in visitors to the House of the Virgin Mary in Ephesus. Many Muslims go to the House of Mary when they have great worries, for example due to incurable diseases, unemployment and an inability to find a spouse. They present their cares and wishes to the Virgin Mary and expect her to intercede with God on their behalf. From their perspective the great Creator will not refuse a request from such a beloved believer, and that is why prayers here are fulfilled if they are offered up with unshakeable faith and honesty.'[76]

Few Christians – too few, especially in Europe – are aware of the extent to which Muslims share their veneration of Mary within the theological boundaries I have defined here. An eyewitness wrote about a visit to this site in June 2000 and was impressed by the devotion shown by Muslims. He had come to the place with his Turkish Muslim travel guide:

The road that winds in hairpin bends up the steep mountainside offers stunning views out over the countryside. Almost nothing has changed here since the Crucifixion of Jesus, with the exception of a few

asphalt roads and busloads of tourists. Shepherds
and goatherds roam with their flocks through the
mountains, as they have done for millennia; the grey-
green olive trees planted on terraces have borne fruit
since time immemorial, and the clothing of the men
and women working in the fields is coarse and plain,
as they have always been. We seem to be driving into
a scene from the Bible, which may remain this way
until the end of time.

We are now approaching the mountain of Mary
after a long period of silence. When we reach the top,
we get out of the bus and walk the rest of the way to
the chapel. The restaurant and the souvenir shops for
tourists disturb the peace and the sweeping panorama
a little, but soon we have left the hubbub of the tourists
behind us and unexpectedly come across a group
celebrating an open-air service. They have erected
an altar, and about one hundred people are kneeling
on the ground, among them dark-skinned Turks from
the East, women in coarsely woven black robes and
pilgrims from Istanbul and Europe. The spot is filled
with a deep sense of peace and inner quietness, and I
long to kneel down next to the others. 'Come,' says our
guide Sedat, 'first we'll go and see Mary!'

The stone chapel is very small and surrounded by
gnarled old trees. It is cool and dim inside. The many
candles give off a homely light. Every candle is a small
token of love, a reflection of the faithful's longing and

hope. We too buy a few candles at the entrance, light them and place them carefully in the wall niches.

Sedat stands in front of the altar, bowing deeply in prayer. He prays with such devotion that he notices none of what is going on around him. I have only ever seen one other such display of piousness, in the Orthodox churches of Kostroma, on the far side of the Volga, where women pray to the icon of the Mother of God in pain and absorption.

When we come out of the chapel, we see a long stone wall stretching out before us. Countless slips of paper bearing the wishes of the pilgrims who come here are vaguely reminiscent of the Western Wall in Jerusalem – sometimes erroneously known as the Wailing Wall – where pious Jews gather and slip their wishes into the cracks so that an angel may come and carry them up into God's sight.[77]

Benedict XVI's visit to the House of Mary in 2006

Pope Benedict XVI insisted on coming to Ephesus during his trip to Turkey in November 2006, and on 29 November he celebrated Mass in the 'Mary Mother House'. In his homily the Pope first reminded the congregation of his predecessors' visits and then of the fact that the future Pope John XXIII, Angelo Roncalli, was papal nuncio in Turkey from January 1935 to December 1944. To quote Benedict XVI: 'He [Angelo Roncalli] very much esteemed and admired the Turkish people. Here I would like to quote an entry in his *Journal of a Soul*: "I love the Turks; I appreciate the natural qualities of these people who have their own place reserved in the march of civilisation" (pp. 233–4). He also left to the Church and the world the legacy of his Christian optimism, rooted in deep faith and constant union with God. In that same spirit, I turn to this nation and, in a special way, to the "little flock" of Christ living in its midst, in order to offer a word of encouragement and to manifest the affection of the whole Church.'[78]

Benedict XVI also knows that Mary, in his words, 'is loved and venerated also by Muslims', particularly on this spot near Ephesus. This allows him to express an impressive call for freedom at the end of his homily: 'Christ "came to proclaim peace" (Eph. 2:17), not only between Jews and non-Jews, but between all nations, since all have their origin in the same God, the one Creator and Lord of the universe. Strengthened by God's word, from here in Ephesus, a city blessed by the presence of Mary Most Holy – who we know is loved and venerated also by Muslims – *let us lift up to the Lord a special prayer for peace between peoples*. From this edge of the Anatolian peninsula, a natural bridge between continents, let us implore peace and reconciliation, above all for those dwelling in the Land called "Holy" and considered as such by Christians, Jews and Muslims alike: it is the land of Abraham, Isaac and Jacob, destined to be the home of a people that would become a blessing for all the nations (cf. Gen 12:1–3). Peace for all of humanity! May Isaiah's prophecy soon be fulfilled: "They shall beat their swords into ploughshares, and their spears into pruning hooks; nation shall not lift up sword against nation, neither shall they learn war any more" (Isa. 2:4). We all need this universal peace; and the Church is called to be not only the prophetic herald, but even more, the "sign and instrument" of this peace.'

How modern Muslim women see Mary

It is also notable how modern-day Muslim theologians and religious education teachers interpret Mary. A book entitled *Der Koran für Kinder und Erwachsene* (*The Qur'an for Children and Adults*) came out in 2008 in a translation and with a commentary by two Muslim religious education teachers, Lamya Kaddor and Rabeya Müller. It is based on the same kind of religious research that is also used for present-day children's Bibles. It was written with the aim, as the authors say, of 'countering a widespread lack of knowledge about their own religion among Muslim children and teenagers' and also of giving 'non-Muslims a guiding thread by which to read the Qur'an'. The goal is to show respect for the Qur'an, but in a 'comprehensible and accessible' form.[79]

How Muslim R.E. teachers interpret Mary for the next generation is of significance to us. What we discover is that Mary is presented as a brave and bold woman, who goes her own way with God's guidance, an independent non-conformist at odds with her social environment; a woman who has to find her destiny and come through her own battles. It is no coincidence that the title of the corresponding chapter sets the tone: 'The Courage to Resist'. Here I will reproduce the (relatively short) text without any further comment:

> Women are not generally mentioned by name in the Qur'an. One major exception is Maryam (Mary). There is even a whole sura, number 19, named after her. Maryam is the prototype of an independent woman. At an early age she feels a spiritual bond with the Creator, and she charts her own path in this relationship. She does unusual things for her sex and for her time. For example, she withdraws from society and, to a degree, from her family. At first she also resists the angel that appears to her and announces the Creator's will to her. She is told that she will have a child without a male partner, talks with the angel and, trusting in God, eventually agrees. She knows full well that ideas about marriage and a woman's role at the time mean that she might pay with her life for the birth of a child she has not conceived by her husband.
>
> She also copes with giving birth alone and gives some sense, through her words, of how hard this must

have been. But even now her trust in God remains unshakeable, as it does when she returns to her people.

Things initially happen as she had predicted they would. She is attacked and comes close to being condemned. Again she trusts in God, and the newborn child speaks out and rescues her. This miracle saves her life, as it convinces her family that divine will is at work.

All of this takes great courage. The Qur'an defines Maryam's son in terms of her own elevated status, not the other way around. Muslims call Isa 'Isa, son of Maryam'.[80]

PART FIVE

The Birth of Jesus in the Qur'an

> We breathed into her [Mary] from Our Spirit and made her
> and her son a sign for all people.
>
> Sura 21:91

> When Jesus was born the devils came to Satan and said,
> 'Today the idols have all lowered their heads.' Satan said,
> 'Something has happened in your world.' Satan flew all
> over the world, but he found nothing. At last he found
> the child Jesus, surrounded by angels. He returned to the
> devils and said, 'Yesterday a prophet was born. No woman
> but she has ever conceived and given birth to a child when
> I was not present. So, after this night, give up all hope
> of idolatry. From now on, lead men into temptation by
> exploiting their imprudence and superficiality.'
>
> Aby Hamid al-Ghazali († 1111)[81]

We can already discern the profile of Jesus, obliquely, through the texts about Mary. Now we want to bring it into focus by studying direct statements about him. This means that we must return to Sura 19, the first major Qur'anic text about Jesus. It is no accident that Jesus is always referred to in the Qur'an by his matronym, Ibn Maryam – 'son of Mary' – 'an obviously polemically motivated "transposition" of his Christian title "son of God", which already signals his exclusively inner-worldly role in the Qur'an. His life story is told in fragmentary fashion: separate reports are scattered throughout the Qur'an and do not crystallise into a precise life story such as that of Moses'.[82]

1. The birth of Jesus as a 'sign from God': Mecca, Sura 19

We have examined the structure, style and basic message of Sura 19, including the backstory of the birth of Jesus centred on John, the son of Zachariah; the sending of the spirit of God to Mary and the dialogue with Mary; and Mary's withdrawals, as she prepares herself utterly to receive God.

Conceived by God's creative power

We have also already established that in the Qur'an the origin of Jesus lies not in male virility and therefore human strength, but in divine force. There is nothing mythological about the conception of Jesus in his mother's womb, and a spiritual intervention is merely hinted at, but what is clear is that Mary's son only exists because he is an expression of God's will: 'I am but a Messenger from your

Lord,' says the spirit of God, who appears to Mary as a 'perfected man', 'come to announce to you the gift of a pure son' (19:19). A *gift*. It is therefore as the gift, and at the initiative, of God alone that Jesus is born. In the Qur'an he is and remains, from the outset, *ibn Maryam*, the son of Mary, and at the same time *rasul Allah*, God's messenger, announced to his mother by a God-sent harbinger. Those words are used of no other prophet or messenger of God in the Qur'an, so let us now take a closer look at this passage.

According to Sura 19, the contractions that set in after Mary's withdrawal to a 'distant place' (Sura 19:22) drive the highly pregnant woman to the trunk of a palm tree. Mary is scared stiff and wishes she had been 'forgotten'. Her ordeal is the same as that of anyone who knows that God has chosen them: fear and hardship. Personal weakness and fragility make a person unworthy to undertake God's bidding, but then come reassuring words: 'But a voice cried to her from below' (Sura 19:24). Who is speaking here?

Consoling words from the new-born baby to its mother

Is it again the angel who had been communicating with Mary earlier? Or is it already the new-born – or perhaps even unborn – baby Jesus? Some translations opt to keep the ambiguity: 'But a voice cried out to her from below'

(Alan Jones: 'And one cried out to her from below'). Rudi Paret's German translation, on the other hand, decides to introduce the baby Jesus, still in his mother's womb, as the subject here: 'He [i.e. the boy Jesus] cried out to her from below.' This interpretation is potentially supported by the Qur'an itself, which later goes on to specify: 'Jesus, son of Mary! Remember My favour to you and to your mother: how I strengthened you with the holy spirit, so that you spoke to people in your infancy and as a grown man' (Sura 5:109). If it is true that the speaker in Sura 19:24 is the newborn infant (which strikes me as plausible in view of Sura 19:30), then this would be the very first instance of the Qur'an putting words in Jesus' mouth:

24 'Do not worry: your Lord has provided a stream at your feet

25 and, if you shake the trunk of the palm tree towards you, it will deliver fresh ripe dates for you,

26 so eat, drink, be glad, and say to anyone you may see: "I have vowed to the Lord of Mercy to abstain from conversation, and I will not talk to anyone today."'

27 She went back to her people carrying the child, and they said, 'Mary! You have done something terrible!

28 Sister of Aaron! Your father was not an evil man; your mother was not unchaste!'

29 She pointed at him. They said, 'How can we
   converse with an infant?'

(Sura 19:24–29)

We should take some time to absorb the fact that the first
words from Jesus in the Qur'an are words of comfort for
his fearful mother – an act that saves her life, designed to
give this woman back her cheer and as a clever piece of
practical advice for the imminent accusations to which
her people will subject her. The newborn child is obviously already aware of the chastisement that Mary can
expect as an unmarried woman with child, and so he
recommends that she fast and remain silent to preserve
her reputation. This spares Mary the need to justify herself
to society, something that would be impossible for her to
do on human terms, just as the Prophet Muhammad was
unable to justify being chosen by God. Also, her son's
words fulfil the divine annunciation that Jesus would be 'a
sign to all men', a sign of God's 'mercy' (19:21), giving rise
to a widespread name for God during the middle Meccan
period: ar-rahman, the 'All-Merciful'.

What is meant by Jesus being 'a servant of God'?

We shall follow Sura 19 a little further, for the figure
of Jesus comes into even sharper focus in the next
section:

30 He said: 'I am a servant of God. He has granted me
   the Scripture; made me a prophet;

31 made me blessed wherever I may be. He
   commanded me to pray, to give alms as long as I
   live,

32 to cherish my mother. He did not make me
   domineering or graceless.

33 Peace was on me the day I was born, and will be
   on me the day I die and the day I am raised to life
   again.'

34 Such was Jesus, son of Mary. [This is] a statement
   of the Truth about which they are in doubt:

35 it would not befit God to have a child. He is far
   above that: when He decrees something, He says
   only, 'Be,' and it is.

36 'God is my Lord and your Lord, so serve Him: that
   is a straight path.'

37 But factions have differed among themselves. What
   suffering will come to those who obscure the truth
   when a dreadful Day arrives!

38 How sharp of hearing, how sharp of sight they will
   be when they come to Us, although now they are
   clearly off course!

(Sura 19:30–38)

Jesus' first description of himself is as a 'servant' of
God. This sounds innocuous, but we should not underes-
timate it as a statement of intent – in both its component

parts. The intent is only clear, however, if the reader immediately reads the opposing statement in parallel: if God had had 'a child', that would mean that there was, alongside God, a 'son' or a 'daughter' of God, a divine or semi-divine being alongside God. From the very start, the Qur'an therefore speaks through Jesus to deny that there is any other divine being beside God: 'I am a servant of God,' with the stress on servant, meaning: I am no son of the gods (in the pagan/polytheistic sense), and also no son of God (in the Christian sense).

This is largely because God has granted Jesus a Holy Book (see Sura 19:30) and has thus made him a special prophet (*nabi* in Arabic). As we have heard, only four people in the entire Qur'an enjoy this status: Moses was given the Torah, David the Psalms, Muhammad the Qur'an and Jesus the Gospels. In other places in the Qur'an, the special status of Jesus is underscored by the fact that he is called not a prophet but a 'Messenger' of God (*rasul* in Arabic) (Suras 4:157 and 171: 5:75). As a result, God can also make Jesus 'blessed' (19:31) – a statement prepared in the same Sura 19 by the formulation that Jesus is 'a sign' of God's 'mercy' to all men (19:21). Greater precision is now supplied: Jesus is a gift of God's boundless blessings. His coming, wherever it may be, is a redemptive and beneficent event. This is an important point for a modern-day dialogue with Muslims about the possibility or impossibility of a 'Qur'anic Christology'. The Münster-based Muslim theologian Mouhanad Khorchide put it this way: 'Jesus' description of himself as a servant of God (19:30) is a key message of the Qur'an. Jesus is the illustration that God works through men, and that men are therefore a medium for the accomplishment of God's intention to communicate his love and mercy. The actions of Jesus in the Qur'an show that by describing himself as a "servant of God", Jesus saw himself as just such a medium and had thus acknowledged his role. The message to Muhammad's audience here is that everybody should follow the example of Jesus and strive as far as possible to be a medium for the achievement of God's intention to bring love and mercy'.[83]

This is also supported by the fact that God commanded Jesus in 19:31 to 'pray' and 'give alms'. It is well known that prayer and alms-giving are two of the five 'pillars' of Islam. From the very beginning, those who believe in the Qur'an stand out from those around them by regularly praying and giving alms. So, by showing Jesus praying and giving alms, the Qur'an presents him as a model Muslim before Islam. This is further emphasised by the fact that God commanded Jesus to 'cherish' his mother, showing Mary particular veneration (19:32). John too had been acknowledged as 'devout and kind to his parents' and 'not domineering or rebellious' earlier in the same sura (Sura 19:13–14).

Not 'domineering or graceless'

These same qualities are now ascribed to Jesus: not 'domineering or graceless'! The terminology employed in Sura 19:32–33 ('He did not make me domineering or graceless. Peace was on me') arouse memories among Christians of Mary's song of praise (the 'Magnificat') and the hymn the angels sing to the shepherds in the Gospel of Luke (Luke 1:46–55; 2:14). There too, Jesus was contrasted with the 'mighty' and the 'rich'. There too, his arrival announced the coming of God's 'peace' on earth.

The Iranian scholar Mehdi Bazargan, respected for his contributions to Christian-Muslim dialogue, comments on this passage in his important book *Der Koran und die Christen* (*And Jesus is His Prophet: The Qur'an and Christians*), published in Germany in 2006:

Jesus' words in 19:32 ('He didn't make me domineering or graceless') sums up his message by explicitly distancing him from tyrants and despots. In the context of the time, this sentence is extremely powerful and significant. The monotheistic religions differentiated themselves sharply from the tyranny and oppression of the Roman Empire, and the fact that the prevailing methods of the forms and systems of rule at the time were no more than aggression and oppression. For that reason, it is almost as if the central message of Jesus Christ and other prophets was not to act tyrannically towards people. It also seems as if this command is a requirement for civilised society and in particular for the faithful (p. 41).

We have already seen that the dialectics of strength and weakness are a constant theme in the line of prophets in the Qur'an, which includes Noah, Abraham and Moses, all of them lone fighters, rejected by their peers, devoid of external strength (weapons and followers). Jesus also belongs to this line. His strength too is his trust in God, not weapons, money or followers.

Yet we should pay attention to the blessing in Sura 19:33 too: 'Peace was on me ...' This is notable for two reasons. The first is that it differs from a similar blessing in the John sura only a few verses earlier. God used the following words about John: 'Peace was on him the day he was born, the day he died, and it will be on him the day he is raised to life again!' (Sura 19:15). God has Jesus himself say, 'Peace was on me the day I was born, and will be on me the day I die and the day I am raised to life again' (Sura 19:33). Muslim exegetes noticed this distinction early on, but they did not play the two off against each other.

The second notable aspect is that the Qur'an has Jesus repeating the creation-theological triad of birth, death and resurrection, as if it were self-evident. What we register above all else is that Jesus pronounces a message about his own death. Sura 4:157 will make it clear that this is far from obvious, as it explicitly rules out Jesus' death on the cross. We will investigate this further in chapter four of the sixth section of the book.

For the time being, though, let us concentrate on an exegesis of Sura 19 and record a significant point of agreement with the representation of Jesus in the New Testament: Jesus is blessed by God and a contrast to all 'domineering' men; he is a man of peace, and this throughout his life – from birth to death, and then to new life with God. We should consciously study the wording of Sura 19:32 again: 'He [God] did not make me domineering.' (Alan Jones translates this as 'overweening'.) What real-life experiences of the intended audience of the Qur'an are suggested by this rejection of 'domineering' rulers? This decisive rejection reminds Christians of Jesus, as a small child, being the polar opposite of a brutal and violent ruler like Herod in the Gospel of Matthew. Matthew's Gospel then makes this idea even clearer, for Jesus is the non-violent king of peace (Matt. 11:28–30; 21: 1–7). This in turns evokes a further similarity. In the birth stories of both the Qur'an and the New Testament, Jesus is God's messenger and he is contrasted with all the mighty, the rich and the tyrannical of the world. Jesus, it is stressed, is not 'domineering' or 'overweening'! If we turn this around, we understand that anyone who is domineering or overweening or a tyrant, of whatever stripe and origin, can lay no claim to Jesus. This son of Mary embodies 'God's peace' on earth.

It would not befit God to have a child

Jesus' presentation of himself in Sura 19:34–36 is immediately followed by a completely different message:

> 34 Such was Jesus, son of Mary. [This is] a statement of the Truth about which they are in doubt:
> 35 it would not befit God to have a child. He is far above that: when He decrees something, He says only, 'Be,' and it is.
> 36 God is my Lord and your Lord, so serve Him: that is a straight path.
> 37 But factions have differed among themselves. What suffering will come to those who obscure the truth when a dreadful Day arrives!
>
> (Sura 19:34–37)

This change of voice sets these verses apart from what has come before, for here the Qur'an does not have Mary or Jesus speak, but God himself. He dictates invasively, imperiously – in a sense 'from above' – who Jesus is and who God is or isn't: 'It would not befit God to have a child.' God is above that; the God revealed in the Qur'an does not stoop to the level of pagan gods. This statement is so important that its negative consequences are conjured up in almost apocalyptic terms at the end of Sura 19:

> 88 The disbelievers say, 'The Lord of Mercy has offspring.'

89 How terrible is this thing you assert:

90 it almost causes the heavens to be torn apart, the
   earth to split asunder, the mountains to crumble to
   pieces,

91 that they attribute offspring to the Lord of Mercy.

(Sura 19:88–91)

So here the 'son of Mary' is 'no longer merely a sign of
God's mercy (19:21) but the subject of a dispute (19:34)',
Angelika Neuwirth writes about this passage. 'This is
taking place with an opposing group, which obviously
counts Jesus among a pantheon – an assumption that is
countered with the argument that God can create anything, immediately, by the power of his word alone and
therefore does not need to conceive a child (19:35) [...]
The dispute about the nature of Jesus is not just taking
place in the present but took place in the past as well,
leading to a schism when he died (19:37). These statements about Jesus do not yet constitute a polemic about
the tenets of the Christian faith, but are still part of a
dispute with pagan adversaries, as a comparison with
Sura 43 shows.'[84]

It is true that we should read Suras 19 and 43 in close
association, since wording from Sura 19 related to Jesus
crops up again in Sura 43, which was written only slightly
later.[85] This would explain why verses 34–36 appear to
have been so abruptly incorporated into the existing narrative and dialogue. It is also striking that 43:81 rejects

the possibility of God having offspring as vehemently as 19:35 and 19:88 do: 'If the Lord of Mercy [truly] had off-spring I would be the first to worship [them],' is its ironic comment on the absurdity of this idea. The passage about the disagreeing factions in Sura 43:65 is also identical to the one in 19:37. And indeed, these 'factions' are not Christian groups but rather pagan opponents of the Prophet, as illustrated by the statement: 'When the son of Mary is cited as an example, your people laugh and jeer, saying, "Are our gods better or him?"' (43:57–58).

The 'pagan Meccans' must have signaled their 'levelling down of the special status of Jesus' as a 'rival to their gods'[86]; and conversely, the first Muslims must have made it plain that although they regard Jesus as the 'servant of God', they will not accept a heavenly family. This also had to be clarified in Sura 19 through the addition of the authoritative verses 19:34–36 in order to dispel any suspicion that the community might accept the son of Mary – created by the spirit of God and able to utter words of comfort to his mother immediately after his birth – as the son of God. When Sura 19:34 stresses 'Such was Jesus, son of Mary' ('Isa bin Maryam'), then this is on the one hand a conscious reworking of the Christian use of the title 'son of God' for Jesus, and at the same time a bulwark against any attempt to turn Jesus into more than a servant, more than a messenger, a bringer of good fortune, a peacemaker for God. No, 'it does not befit God to have a child' (Sura 19:35; see also Suras 2:116; 4:171; 9:30).

We do, however, wish to note that the Qur'an does not use the word 'son' (*ibnun* in Arabic) at this and other points, but instead the more general term 'child' (*waladun* in Arabic). This strengthens the previously discussed suspicion (Part 1, Chapter 5) that the Qur'an obviously rejects all primitive ideas of divine children – for example, mythological notions of a sexual relationship between a god and a woman leading to the conception of a child. The Qur'an clearly assumes a familiarity with the mythological idea of 'divine childhood', and thus the idea of a polytheistic pantheon of divine fathers, mothers and children. This is understandable: the Prophet was familiar, from an environment bearing the imprint of ancient Near Eastern polytheism, with a host of such divine sons and daughters, who lured humans into idolatrous practices.

This is anathema to the Qur'an – anathema for the sake of the One True God! In the Qur'an's conception of religion, attributing 'a child' or even children to God would equate to dividing God and damaging God's unity. As if there could be a second 'God' or even several godlike beings alongside the one God! 'Associating' (*shirk* in Arabic) is the taboo word for this in the Qur'an. 'Associating' other beings as equal partners with God is an unforgivable sin in the Qur'an (see Sura 4:48 and 116). For 'He [God] begot no one nor was He begotten,' it says in the early Meccan period (Sura 112). This is reinforced at the crucial point in Sura 19 by additional words attributed to Jesus: 'God is my Lord and your Lord, so serve Him: that is a straight path' (Sura 19:36). Jesus' statement that he is the 'servant of God' means in substance that God alone is his 'Lord'. Here, for the first time, according to Mehdi Bazargan, we have 'before our eyes a rejection of the claim that God joined a son to himself. This rejection is based on the argument that a creator who can realise any desire to create something through his pure will, can have no need of a son or helper'.[87]

An heir to the great Prophets

The Qur'an's conception of Jesus as the messenger of God is consolidated over time, so much so that by the late Meccan period Jesus can appear quite naturally as one of a line of great prophets whom God sent to humankind. This explains why the (relatively few) statements about Jesus after Sura 19 are – and can be – mainly in serial form. This is true of both Sura 6 and Sura 42:

84 We gave him Isaac and Jacob, each of whom
    We guided, as We had guided Noah before, and
    among his descendants were David, Solomon, Job,
    Joseph, Moses, and Aaron – in this way We reward
    those who do good –
85 Zachariah, John, Jesus, and Elijah – every one of
    them was righteous.

(Sura 6:84)

13 In matters of faith, He has laid down for you
[people] the same commandment that He
gave Noah, which We have revealed to you
[Muhammad] and which We enjoined on Abraham
and Moses and Jesus: 'Uphold the faith and do not
divide into factions within it.'

(Sura 42:13)

2. Controversy about Jesus: Medina, Sura 3

We shall now switch to Sura 3 from the Medina period.
We have already noted that the accounts of the annunciation and birth of John and Mary had been taken up again.
We also identified the reasons for this: John and Mary
were considered members of the Jewish people, and their
depiction as prototypical believers was intended as a criticism of the resistance of the contemporary 'children of
Israel'. As we have already heard, the longer the Medina
period lasted, the more bitter the dispute between the
Prophet and the three Jewish tribes who lived in the city
became.

What the angels tell Mary about Jesus

That also had an impact on the representation of Jesus.
Immediately after the angel's annunciation to Mary (Sura
3:42–44), Sura 3 states:

45 The angels said, 'Mary, God gives you news of a
   Word from Him, whose name will be the Messiah,
   Jesus, son of Mary, who will be held in honour in
   this world and the next, who will be one of those
   brought near to God.

46 He will speak to people in his infancy and in his
   adulthood. He will be one of the righteous.

48 He will teach him the Scripture and wisdom, the
   Torah and the Gospel,

49 He will send him as a messenger to the Children of
   Israel.'

                                    (Sura 3:45–46; 48–49)

Two key statements catch our attention here. In Sura 3:45
the Qur'an calls Jesus 'the Messiah' and 'Word from Him',
i.e. 'Word of God'. It is well known that Christians link
these two words to a belief in Jesus' central role in the story
of salvation and revelation, both towards Jews ('Christ' is
the Greek translation of the Hebrew word 'Messiah' or
'the Anointed One') and towards Greeks ('logos'). It is a
central Christian tenet that the 'Word of God' (*logos theou*
in Greek) was made 'flesh' (*sarx* in Greek) in a fashion
unique in history: *logos sarx egeneto* (John 1:14). Is this
what Sura 3:45 means here? Hardly. Jesus does not play
a central role in the Qur'an. The essential thing for the
Qur'an is the Qur'an itself. In Sura 3:45 'Messiah' is used
explicitly as a 'name' for Jesus, who is again – pointedly –
called 'son of Mary'. 'Messiah' is therefore not meant as a

'distinction' in recognition of his centrality to the history of salvation (as it is in the New Testament), but as a proper noun, which is nonetheless a sign of something special.

We should mention these signs objectively in conversations with Muslims, but we should neither appropriate them 'Christologically' nor denigrate them and play them down. This does, however, constitute a major theological signal to the Jewish community. Indeed, only a few lines later in Sura 3:49 Jesus is described as a 'messenger to the Children of Israel'. This statement is lent further weight by the fact that God teaches Jesus a comprehensive knowledge of Scripture – the Torah and the Gospel (Sura 3:48). Jesus may not have a central supra-historical role but, compared with other prophets, Sura 3 does assign him a special *historical* position – both in this world *and* the next. In this world he is able to speak, even as an infant (Sura 3:46 quotes Sura 19:19 almost verbatim), and as an adult he is one of the 'righteous' – a prestigious title given in the Qur'an to those who devoutly obey God's word. He is special in the next world because he is 'brought near to God'.

How the Qur'an interprets Jesus' miracles

It is a similar matter when it comes to the description of Jesus in Sura 3:45 as the 'Word of Him'. The Qur'an then illustrates this by means of the so-called bird miracle, which follows in Sura 3:49.

49 He will send him as a messenger to the Children
    of Israel: 'I have come to you with a sign from
    your Lord: I will make the shape of a bird for you
    out of clay, then breathe into it and, with God's
    permission, it will become a real bird; I will heal
    the blind and the leper, and bring the dead back
    to life with God's permission; I will tell you what
    you may eat and what you may store up in your
    houses. There truly is a sign for you in this, if you
    are believers.
50 I have come to confirm the truth of the Torah
    which preceded me, and to make some things
    lawful to you which used to be forbidden.
    I have come to you with a sign from your
    Lord.'

                                    (Sura 3:49–50)

There are tangible parallels here with the New Testament
accounts of the 'miraculous deeds' of Jesus, for example
in Luke's Gospel:

  And he came down with them, and stood in the
  plain, and the company of his disciples, and a great
  multitude of people out of all Judaea and Jerusalem,
  and from the sea coast of Tyre and Sidon, which came
  to hear him, and to be healed of their diseases; And
  they that were vexed with unclean spirits: and they
  were healed. And the whole multitude sought to touch

him: for there went virtue out of him, and healed them all.

(Luke 6:17–19)

There are also parallels with Jesus' 'miracles' such as the healing of the blind (Matt. 12:22) and the raising of the dead (Mark 5:35–43; Luke 7:11–17; John 11:39–44). We should note that the Qur'an does not refer to 'spectacular' miracles by Jesus (the calming of the storm, the transformation of water into wine: Mark 4:35–41; John 2:1–11), but rather ones that benefit the weak, the sick and the powerless in society, such as the blind, lepers and the deceased. This confirms that Jesus is a further sign of God's 'mercy' in the Qur'an.

There is also a Christian parallel to the bird miracle mentioned in Sura 3:49 (the bringing to life of a bird made of clay), though not in the New Testament. It is to be found in non-canonical Christian literature, in the text known as the Infancy Gospel of Thomas, which has been dated to the end of the second century:

This little child Jesus when he was five years old was playing at the ford of a brook [...] And having made soft clay, he fashioned thereof twelve sparrows. And it was the Sabbath when he did these things. And there were also many other little children playing with him. And a certain Jew when he saw what Jesus did, playing upon the Sabbath day, departed straightway and told his father Joseph: 'Lo, thy child is at the brook, and he hath taken clay and fashioned twelve little birds, and hath polluted the Sabbath day.'

And Joseph came to the place and saw: and cried out to him, saying: 'Wherefore doest thou these things on the Sabbath, which it is not lawful to do?'

But Jesus clapped his hands together and cried out to the sparrows and said to them: 'Go!' and the sparrows took their flight and went away chirping.

And when the Jews saw it they were amazed, and departed and told their chief men that which they had seen Jesus do.[88]

Once more, it is helpful to undertake close intertextual comparison in order to bring the content into sharper focus. The Christian miracle stories describe a conflict between Jesus and his traditional Jewish environment. They illustrate how Jesus serenely broke the Sabbath taboo as a child while carrying out miracles. The Qur'an also mentions the bird miracle in the context of a dispute with contemporary Judaism. Yet, in the Qur'an, Jesus is if not an exclusive, then at least a special sign, due to his exceptional abilities: he spoke as a new-born baby, and performs further miracles growing up. It is clear that there can be no claims to exclusivity in any salvation historical sense, because the miraculous signs that Jesus gives, according to the Qur'an, take place expressly 'with God's permission'. Here too, therefore, we are confronted with a theocentric rather than a Christological message – it is a further sign 'from your Lord!'

A precise comparison of the various texts establishes a crucial difference between the Islamic and the Christian miracle stories. In the Christian accounts, it is Jesus himself who has the strength within himself to carry out the miraculous deeds. The Qur'an, on the other hand, always emphasises the 'divine leave' that allows Jesus to act. It is no accident that Sura 3:49 twice mentions 'God's permission', with which Jesus achieves his extraordinary deeds. Once again, this example demonstrates the difference between Christ-centred and theocentric portrayals of Jesus. Jesus' deeds do not stress his own power, but rather the creative power of God acting *through* him. Jesus is therefore truly 'the prototype for God acting through a human being', embodying 'in ideal fashion, the accomplishment of God's intention to communicate his love and mercy through a human being. Being filled with the spirit helps him to obey perfectly the divine inspiration of the spirit of God within a person, which is why the Qur'an is described as both the Word and the Spirit of God (see 4:171). All of these things are a mark of special distinction on Jesus'.[89]

A short summary of the Qur'an's representation of Jesus

There are relatively few statements about Jesus' acts in the

Qur'an. It is therefore all the more remarkable when Sura 5 returns to the subject, but this time not in a speech by Jesus, but in a speech by God:

109 On the Day when God assembles all the messengers and asks, 'What response did you receive?' they will say, 'We do not have that knowledge: You alone know things that cannot be seen.'

110 Then God will say, 'Jesus, son of Mary! Remember My favour to you and to your mother: how I strengthened you with the holy spirit, so that you spoke to people in your infancy and as a grown man; how I taught you the Scripture and wisdom, the Torah and the Gospel; how, by My leave, you fashioned the shape of a bird out of clay, breathed into it, and it became, by My leave, a bird; how, by My leave, you healed the blind person and the leper; how, by My leave, you brought the dead back to life; how I restrained the Children of Israel from [harming] you when you brought them clear signs, and those of them who disbelieved said, "This is clearly nothing but sorcery";

111 and how I inspired the disciples to believe in Me and My messengers – they said, "We believe and bear witness that we devote ourselves [to God]."'

(Sura 5:109–111)

This text can be considered a short summary of how Jesus is represented in the Qur'an, especially since, as is widely known, Sura 5 is chronologically the last sura in the Qur'an. Verse 109 establishes the leitmotiv of the following section: God's messengers, assembled for Judgment Day, have no knowledge of the outcome of their assignment. They 'know nothing', and they place their full trust in God, who is the only one who knows 'things that cannot be seen'. This also applies to Jesus, although as the subsequent passage explains, he has been in God's 'favour' since his birth.

This short summary is a compilation of the favours God has bestowed on Jesus, summarised *by* God *in* a direct speech to Jesus. The text underlines these two aspects with the utmost clarity. In the Qur'an, Jesus is nothing on his own; he owes everything to God. Yet at the same time, God acts through Jesus in the world, through his deeds and signs, and he does this in a way that set Jesus apart from other prophets. In comparison to them he is unique from his birth to his death and on to the Final Judgment (see Suras 16:84–89 and 4:41, 159). Although this does not make him unique in the history of salvation, it does make him historically preeminent.

The first statement in Sura 5:109–111 refers to the circumstances of Jesus' birth – Mary's encounter with the spirit and the breath of the spirit in her; and Jesus' ability to speak as a newborn, as set out in Suras 19:17, 66:12 and 19:29. The second statement again lists the 'miraculous

deeds' of Jesus, with which we are familiar from Sura
3:49. The accent here too is on 'God's permission'. The
third statement ('restrained the Children of Israel') takes
up the theme of Sura 4:157 – protecting Jesus from the
shameful death on the cross, visited upon him by the Jews
(more on this in Chapter 4 in this section). The fourth statement highlights the fact that Jesus' disciples can already
be regarded as 'devout'; they are 'Muslims' before Islam
even exists.[90]

This is the obvious message of Jesus' representation in
the Qur'an, which hardened during the Medina period. It
is intended to teach the 'Children of Israel' a lesson by presenting Jesus as a messenger of God, who has sent special
signs. This story is an attack on the prevailing ignorance of
'signs' among Jews in the days of the Prophet. It also takes
aim at their attitude towards all the prophets of Israel prior
to Jesus. The Qur'an accentuates Jesus' symbolic importance in order to heighten people's awareness of the 'sign'
of the final, defining Prophet. We should therefore pay
close attention to the statement at the end of verse 110,
which states that Jesus' destiny is a clear foreshadowing of
the Prophet's fate. Jesus had already provided 'clear signs'
– bringing to life birds fashioned from clay, healing the
blind and the leprous, raising the dead from their graves
– but the unbelievers do not heed them, dismissing them
all as 'sorcery'.

3. Comparing the birth stories

Comparing the accounts in the New Testament and the Qur'an, one finds some notable similarities as well as some essential differences. I shall first give a brief overview of the similarities.

What the New Testament and the Qur'an have in common

We saw that both the New Testament and the Qur'an interpret the birth of Jesus as a miraculous act performed by God for the benefit of humankind. One remarkable aspect is that whereas the New Testament essentially restricts God's miraculous design to the angels' appearances to Zachariah, Mary and the shepherds, along with the astrologers following a star, the Qur'an adds a miraculous speech by the new-born baby. The Qur'an clearly has no scruples about having the new-born baby Jesus speak words of comfort to his mother and utter prophetic statements about himself. And why should it? As with John, it uses the story of the birth of Jesus as a powerful illustration of its central theological tenet.

We can therefore formulate a **first point of consensus** between the New Testament and the Qur'an. *In the birth stories of the New Testament and the Qur'an, God holds sway over the seemingly impossible. God is free in his actions, breaking through all earthly boundaries and human parameters. Old, barren women are made fertile* *again; young women become pregnant without the participation of a man; God creates new life in the empty, dead desert; a newborn child speaks with the force and self-assurance of an adult.*

This leads on to a **second point of consensus** between the New Testament and the Qur'an. *In the birth stories of the New Testament and the Qur'an, God breaks through men's scepticism, doubt and disbelief. The birth of Jesus, especially, stresses that God has the power to make the infertile fertile, the dead come alive, and something from nothing. Both birth stories are theocentric. This is expressed in the New Testament as 'For with God nothing will be impossible' (Luke 1:37), and in the Qur'an, 'When He has ordained something, He only says, "Be", and it is' (Sura 3:47).*

In the birth accounts of the New Testament and the Qur'an, Jesus is 'a spirit from Him' (also in Sura 4:171). He is created by God himself from nothing. He owes the fact that he has been brought to life entirely to God's will and God's actions. This also explains the other 'titles' given to Jesus in the Qur'an: 'servant of God', 'prophet of God', 'Word of God'. All these titles express the same basic idea: Jesus has been marked out by God from the moment of his conception. He is even distinguished from other servants and prophets of God by a special characteristic: he has been created by the spirit of God so that he might use the power of this spirit as God's messenger over his lifetime. In this, Jesus is a unique figure in the Qur'an.

Only Adam surpasses him regarding his origins, since the
Qur'an says that he came into the world without even the
involvement of an earthly mother (Sura 2:30).

This gives rise to a **third point of consensus**. *As in the
New Testament, the accounts of Jesus' birth in the Qur'an
say that he is not the fruit of terrestrial history nor a human
creation: he is a creature of the spirit, a creature of God.
The fact of being a creature of the spirit and the product
of a virgin birth distinguish Jesus from all other prophets and messengers in the Qur'an, including Muhammad
the messenger, whose earthly paternity the Qur'an never
leaves in any doubt. Yet it is precisely his creation by the
spirit that means that Jesus is not an exclusive messenger
in the Qur'an. Creation by the spirit and a virgin birth do
not, as in the New Testament, emphasise the uniqueness
of Jesus, but rather the uniqueness of God.*

Jesus is blessed by God and stands in contrast to the
'domineering and graceless' tyrants. Indeed, he is a man
of peace throughout his earthly existence – from his birth
to his death and on to his new life with God. We should
again take conscious note of the wording of Sura 19:32:
'He [God] did not make me domineering and graceless.'

This establishes a **fourth point of consensus.** *In the
birth stories of both the Qur'an and the New Testament,
Jesus is God's messenger and is contrasted with all the
mighty, the rich and the tyrannical in the world. Jesus,
it is stressed, is not 'domineering' or 'overweening'! If
we turn this around, we understand that anyone who*

is domineering or overweening or a tyrant, of whatever stripe and origin, can lay no claim to Jesus. This son of Mary embodies the 'peace of God' on earth.

Comparing the texts enables us to see just how independently Muhammad managed to interpret Biblical accounts of all sources in accordance with his theological axioms. He adopts them, intensifies them, stringently interprets them and then arranges them to support his overriding theological manifesto – theocentricity, God as the centre of the world and of history. His will permeates everything, and the whole of creation must be understood as a 'sign' (*aya* in Arabic).

We can thus present a **fifth point of consensus** between the Qur'an and the New Testament. *Jesus shows the way of God through his annunciation and his acts. According to the New Testament, God authenticated Jesus 'by miracles, wonders and signs' (Acts 2:22). The Qur'an says something similar: Jesus' deeds (healing the blind and the leprous, raising the dead, etc.) are a 'sign' from God (Sura 3:49). More than that: Jesus is a personal sign from God. The statement in Sura 19:21, by which God seeks to make Jesus 'a sign to all men', a sign of divine 'mercy', is matched by the insight that Luke the Evangelist puts in the mouth of the old Jew Simeon when he meets the newborn boy and his mother Mary in the temple in Jerusalem: 'This Child [...] is a sign that will be spoken against' (Luke 2:34).*

Where the New Testament and the Qur'an differ

Now we turn to where the birth stories of the New Testament and the Qur'an differ in their theological manifestos. We must also analyse this again in the clearest possible terms at the end of our exegesis. We shall highlight the essential distinction by means of a selected scene: Mary's reaction to the annunciation of the birth by God's messenger. Below is an overview of the versions in Luke's Gospel and in the Qur'an, set alongside each other.

Luke 1:26–33	Sura 19:16–21	Sura 3:45–47
Now in the sixth month the angel Gabriel was **sent by God** to a city of Galilee named Nazareth, to a virgin betrothed to a man whose name was Joseph, of the house of David. The virgin's name *was* Mary. And having come in, the angel said to her, 'Rejoice, highly favored *one*, the Lord *is* with you.'	Mention in the Quran the story of Mary [...] We sent Our **Spirit** to appear before her [...] I am but a **Messenger** from your Lord.	The **angels** said, '**Mary, God gives you news** ...'

Luke 1:26–33	Sura 19:16–21	Sura 3:45–47
But when she saw *him* she was **troubled** at his saying, and considered what manner of greeting this was.	'I seek the Lord of Mercy's **protection** against you: if you have any fear of Him.'	
'You will conceive in your womb and bring forth a **Son**.'	'I am but a Messenger from your Lord, [come] to announce to you the gift of a **pure** son.'	
'and shall call His name **Jesus**.'		'God gives you news of a Word from Him, whose name will be the **Messiah, Jesus**.'
'**Son of the Highest**; and the Lord God will give Him the throne of His father David. And He will reign over the house of Jacob forever, and of His kingdom there will be no end.'		'The **son of Mary**, who will be held in honour in this world and the next, who will be one of those brought near to God. He will speak to people in his infancy and in his adulthood. He will be one of the righteous.'

Luke 1:26–33	Sura 19:16–21	Sura 3:45–47
'How can this be, since I **do not know a man?**'	'How can I have a son when **no man has touched me?** I have not been unchaste?'	'My Lord, how can I have a son when **no man has touched me?**'
'The **Holy Spirit** will come upon you, and the **power of the Highest** will overshadow you; therefore, also, that Holy One who is to be born will be called the Son of God. Now indeed, Elizabeth your relative has also conceived a son in her old age; and this is now the sixth month for her who was called barren. For **with God nothing will be impossible.**'	'This is what **your Lord** said: "It is easy for Me." […] And so **it was ordained**.'	'This is how **God creates what He will**: when He has ordained something, He only says, "**Be**", and it is.'

This precise textual comparison highlights the specific profile of Jesus' representations in the New Testament and the Qur'an respectively, and it does so in several respects:

1. In Luke's Gospel, a human narrator speaks ('Now in the sixth month, the angel Gabriel was sent by God …'), whereas in the Qur'an the narrator is divine ('We sent Our Spirit …').

2. In Luke's Gospel, the annunciation of the birth is precisely dated and located. The Qur'an makes no mention of where the apparition takes place, nor does it mention Joseph, Mary's partner. The stories of John and Jesus are not chronologically distinct.

3. In the Qur'an (and in particular in Sura 3), Muhammad's reminder of God's actions relating to Mary and Jesus are part of his dispute with contemporary Judaism, and therefore Israel is never mentioned in the Qur'anic text. The New Testament version also engages with contemporary Judaism, but the objective is to announce the newborn child as the messianic ruler over Israel for Israel's sake, to 'reign over the house of Jacob forever'.

4. In the New Testament, Jesus is explicitly named 'Son of the Highest' (Luke 1:32), which is summed up in the trenchant phrase: 'that Holy One who is to be born will be called the Son of God' (Luke 1:35). Luke's annunciation 'plays' quite deliberately with the ambiguity of the title of 'Son' for Jesus: the son of Mary is at the same time 'Son of the Highest'! The Qur'an avoids the title of son every bit as deliberately. The synoptic opposition

is particularly revealing at this point: instead of 'Son of the Highest' the Qur'an pointedly uses 'son of Mary'!

5. Jesus' pre-eminent position in the Gospel is to bring salvation forever, for all eternity, therefore 'and of His Kingdom there shall be no end'. Jesus also occupies a pre-eminent position in the Qur'an: 'He will speak to the people in his infancy', will be 'held in honour' in this world, is 'one of the righteous', and for that he will be brought near to God in the next world, after his death. Yet Jesus' position in the Qur'an is historically contained, as were those of all the prophets and messengers who came before him.

To recap: that which the Qur'an consciously avoids is essential to the New Testament's key message – the designation of Jesus as the 'Son of God' with a kingdom 'of which there will be no end'. We can boil down the crucial differences between the stories in the Bible and the Qur'an to three points:

In the New Testament accounts, the birth of Jesus is embedded in the history of God's relationship with his chosen people. That is why the birth in Bethlehem is important, why contemporary political rulers are mentioned (Augustus, Herod) and why precise details of the birth story are given a historical context (the homage

paid by the astrologers and the shepherds). On the
contrary, the Qur'an is lifted out of history. It is interested
neither in the specific place of birth or residence of
Jesus (no mention of Bethlehem or Nazareth) nor in the
precise time (no mention of the political rulers at the
time or the circumstances) nor does it mention Joseph,
whom the Bible cites as Jesus' earthly father. It focuses
entirely on God's interaction with individual people
such as Zachariah, Mary and Jesus.

The New Testament sources see Jesus' birth as the
final fulfilment of an ancient prediction to his people,
the eschatological climax of God's devotion to his
people Israel. The coming of Jesus is a new beginning,
brought about by the spirit, a messianic re-start for
Israel and a sign for the conversion of the Gentiles.
In the Qur'an too, God treats Jesus with special
distinction. However, the son of Mary is still a sign
from God – distinctive perhaps, but one of many.

In the New Testament accounts, Jesus of Nazareth
is the ultimate revealer of God to Israel and the
Gentiles; a prophet like John the Baptist merely points
to him. For Muslims, the ultimate revelation of God
exists in the Qur'an, and it is to the Qur'an that all
prophets, including John and Jesus, point. Christology
and Qur'anology correlate. The fundamental difference
between Christianity and Islam is, and remains, that for
Christians, the word of God is made man in Jesus; in
Islam, the word of God is made book in the Qur'an.

What becomes clear is that the more closely one works on and with the sources, the more profound points of consensus one sees between Christian and Muslim beliefs, but also lasting, dividing differences and claims to truth, which in the final analysis throw down the gauntlet to choose one's faith. Both of these must be voiced in any dialogue worthy of the name.

The Qur'an's 'Christmas story' should be read as a model for such a dialogue by Christians and Muslims alike. It challenges followers of both religions to reflect deeply on the secret of God's actions in the story of Jesus, analysing it to extract what they have in common and where they differ. It is not the end of dialogue, but the basis for dialogue. It can teach us to read what unites us in the light of what divides us, and what divides us in the light of what unites us. It could bring about a communicative dialogue, which can go even deeper, for Christians and Muslims must always be aware that they do not 'have', 'manage' or 'possess' the secret of God, but wish to discover more through faith and thought; communication, with mutual respect for final decisions and final beliefs. We shall now analyse this further by returning to the 'signals' we discussed at the start of the book.

PART SIX

A Call for Dialogue

A man came to Jesus and said, 'Teacher of goodness,
teach me something that you know and I do not, that
benefits me and does you no harm.' Jesus asked, 'What
would that be?' The man said, 'How can a servant be
truly pious before God?' Jesus replied, 'The matter is
easy. You must truly love God in your heart and work
in His service, exerting all your effort and strength, and
be merciful toward the people of your race as you show
mercy to yourself.' He said, 'Teacher of goodness, who are
the people of my race?' Jesus replied, 'All the children of
Adam. And that which you do not wish to be done to you,
do not do to others. In this way you will be truly pious
before God.'

Ahmad ibn Hanbal (d. 855)[91]

If Muslims and Christians are not at peace, the world
cannot be at peace [...] So let our differences not cause
hatred and strife between us. Let us vie with each other
only in righteousness and good works. Let us respect each
other, be fair, just and kind to one another and live in
sincere peace, harmony and mutual goodwill.

From *A Common Word between Us and You (2007)*

On 13 October 2007, as we already stated in the prologue, an event took place that was historically unprecedented and therefore quite remarkable. One hundred and
thirty-eight leaders from around the Muslim world wrote
an open letter to the Pope and other representatives of
Christian Churches and communities of believers, urging
them to engage in dialogue with Muslims.

1. A Common Word

That letter was entitled 'A Common Word', a title that had not
been chosen at random. It refers to Sura 3:64 of the Qur'an.
It is a remarkable passage, and it deserves closer study.

The key passage in the Qur'an: Sura 3:64

We are quite familiar with Sura 3 by now. We have examined verses 33–57 about Mary, John and Jesus in detail.
The surprising thing is that from Sura 3:59 onwards, the
Qur'an returns once more to the significance of Jesus, as
if what went before had not adequately clarified the situation. Suddenly the Qur'an states in an authoritarian and
statutory manner:

59 In God's eyes Jesus is just like Adam: He created
   him from dust, said to him, 'Be', and he was.
60 This is the truth from your Lord, so do not be one
   of those who doubt.

61 If anyone disputes this with you now that you have been given this knowledge, say, 'Come, let us gather our sons and your sons, our women and your women, ourselves and yourselves, and let us pray earnestly and invoke God's rejection on those of us who are lying.'

62 This is the truth of the matter: there is no god but God; God is the Exalted, the Decider.

63 If they turn away, [know that] God is well aware of anyone who causes corruption.

64 Say, 'People of the Book, let us arrive at a statement that is common to us all: we worship God alone, we ascribe no partner to Him, and none of us takes others beside God as lords.' If they turn away, say, 'Witness our devotion to Him.'

(Sura 3:59–64)

The surprising thing about this text is not only the repetition of 'In God's eyes Jesus ...' but also the change of audience. This is no longer confined to the 'Children of Israel', for here it speaks to 'People of the Book', which presumably means Christians above all others. The appeal 'Come, let us gather our sons and your sons ...' (Sura 3:61) requires some explanation. This is clearly a summons to a meeting in order to reach 'a common word', as it says later on (Sura 3:64). What is the context for this?

This text has not been dated with any certainty. Was it written before the Battle of Badr in March 624, or only in

631? It is presumed that a delegation of Christians arrived from Najran in northern Yemen. They saw the pressure of the spread of Islam as a threat to their religious, political and economic freedoms and therefore sent a delegation to sound out the situation and negotiate in Medina.[92] The most powerful trading centre in the south of the peninsula must have had an interest in finding out more about the strength, intentions and plans of its northern counterpart.

A model of understanding

Discussions apparently revolve around the true nature of Christ, as well as the foundations of faith. The conversations go nowhere. The Christians from Najran are unable to accept the representation of Jesus in the Qur'an (although Muhammad supposedly does his utmost to point out the links between Christianity and Islam), and the Muslims will not agree to a central tenet of traditional Christology – the divine and human nature of Jesus. Two articles of faith have been dogma for the Orthodox Christian Church since the fifth century: God is understood as one being made up of three persons (the Trinity), and Jesus Christ is regarded as a 'divine' person with two beings, one divine and one human (the doctrine of the two natures of Christ). Since the Council of Chalcedon in 451, Christian doctrine cleaves to the union of *vere Homo* and *vere Deus* in Jesus: true God and true man in a single (divine) person!

After a long period of negotiations, however, the two parties obviously manage to agree on a 'Judgment of God' (Ordal). This is what Sura 3:61 must be referring to when it says: 'Come, let us gather our sons and your sons [...] let us pray earnestly and invoke God's rejection on those of us who are lying.' Both parties state that they are willing to enter into a stable contractual arrangement laying out both their inalienable rights and their duties. The Christians from Najran will not be compelled to adopt Islam, but they are not allowed to pass on their belief in the divine nature of Christ to Muslims. They are, however, granted wide-ranging political and religious autonomy and economic self-sufficiency, and this is sealed with an indissoluble oath and sanctified by the Prophet's word of honour.

Whatever the historical truth regarding this 'agreement', and whatever the historical answer to the question as to whether Sura 3:59–64 is a true reflection of the negotiations around such an 'agreement', in terms of beliefs Sura 3:59 and 3:64 contain key points on which Muslims and Christians were able to agree in principle. The wording regarding the conception of Jesus is as follows: 'In God's eyes Jesus is just like Adam: He created him from dust, said to him, "Be", and he was' (Sura 3:59).

The key points regarding the understanding of God are:

- Serve only one God (positive formulation of monotheism);

- Associate no partner with God (negative formulation of monotheism);
- Worship no man as a god (consequences of monotheism).

This creates a conceptual framework for consensus between Muslims and Christians, no less! One might say that it is a minimal consensus, sketched out in the form of the three key points above, but it obviously served as a basis for a peaceful relationship and mutual recognition between Muslims and Christians in the past. If we understand it properly, this could also be the case in the future.

2. The Document of the 138

In his commentary on the Qur'an, it was no coincidence that Adel Theodor Khoury noted that Sura 3:59–64 had become a 'model' in the Islamic tradition for shaping relations between Muslims and Christians.[93] Its precise importance was demonstrated by the aforementioned document, 'A Common Word', signed and published in October 2007 by 138 Muslim theologians from around the world. This letter picks up on the key statement in Sura 3:64, reproducing the relevant passage at the end of the document. We shall quote the wording again here: 'People of the Book, let us arrive at a statement that is common to us all: we worship God alone, we ascribe no partner to Him, and none of us takes others beside God as lords. If they turn away, say, "Witness our devotion to Him."' The document draws two conclusions from this.

Conclusions for Muslims and Christians

The first conclusion concerns Muslims' conception of themselves. The statement in Sura 3:64 'worship God alone' relates, according to the Document of the 138, to 'being totally devoted to God and hence to the First and Greatest Commandment'. According to one of the earliest and most influential commentaries on the Qur'an, written by al-Tabari (who died in 923 AD), the other formulation 'and none of us takes others beside God as lords' means that no one should disobey God's commandments or worship others by prostrating himself before them as one prostrates oneself before God. Muslims, Christians and Jews should be free to obey what God has commanded them to do and not have to prostrate themselves before kings and other rulers, for God says in the Holy Qur'an: 'There is no compulsion in religion' (Sura 2:256). According to the document, this relates to 'the Second Commandment and to love of the neighbour of which justice and freedom of religion are a crucial part'. Justice and freedom of religion? We listen up when we hear these terms and we shall discuss this statement later.

The second conclusion the document draws is an invitation to Christians to 'remember Jesus' words in the Gospel', for example those in Mark's Gospel: 'The Lord

our God, the Lord is one. And you shall love the Lord
your God with all your heart, with all your soul, with all
your mind and with all your strength. This is the first commandment. And the second, like it, is this: "You shall love
your neighbour as yourself." There is no other commandment greater than these' (Mark 12:29–31). Immediately
after this the document makes a dramatic declaration:

As Muslims, we say to Christians that we are not
against them and that Islam is not against them – so
long as they do not wage war against Muslims on
account of their religion, oppress them and drive them
out of their homes, (in accordance with the verse of
the Holy Qur'an [Al-Mumtahinah, 60:8]) [...]

Is Christianity necessarily against Muslims? In the
Gospel Jesus Christ says: 'He who is not with me is
against me, and he who does not gather with me
scatters abroad' (Matthew 12:30). 'For he who is not
against us is on our side' (Mark 9:40). 'For he who is
not against us is on our side' (Luke 9:50).

According to the Blessed Theophylact's *Explanation
of the New Testament*, these statements are not
contradictions because the first statement (in the actual
Greek text of the New Testament) refers to demons,
whereas the second and third statements refer to
people who recognised Jesus, but were not Christians.
Muslims recognise Jesus Christ as the Messiah, not in
the same way Christians do (but Christians themselves

anyway have never all agreed with each other on Jesus Christ's nature), but in the following way: 'The Messiah Jesus, son of Mary, is a Messenger of God and His Word which he cast unto Mary and a Spirit from Him….' (Al-Nisa', 4:171).

We therefore invite Christians to consider Muslims not against and thus with them, in accordance with Jesus Christ's words here. Finally, as Muslims, and in obedience to the Holy Qur'an, we ask Christians to come together with us on the common essentials of our two religions … that we shall worship none but God, and that we shall ascribe no partner unto Him, and that none of us shall take others for lords beside God … (Al 'Imran, 3:64).

This is an astonishing and historic invitation! It has received serious responses from Christians. For example, Pope Benedict XVI not only welcomed this document, he approved the establishment of a Muslim-Catholic Forum to look more deeply into the questions it raised. As early as 19 November 2007, Benedict XVI asked his state secretary, Cardinal Bertone, to let the signatories know the following: 'Without ignoring or downplaying our differences as Christians and Muslims, we can and therefore should look to what unites us, namely, belief in the one God, the provident Creator and universal Judge who at the end of time will deal with each person according to his or her actions. We are all called to commit ourselves totally to him and to obey his sacred will. Mindful of the content of his Encyclical Letter *Deus Caritas Est* ("God is Love"), His Holiness was particularly impressed by the attention given in the letter to the twofold commandment to love God and one's neighbour.'[94]

Suspicion about the document

Other reactions were less positive. I shall quote statements from two very different 'parties' as examples. Some Islamic scholars accused those who penned the document of having 'no coherent, viable hermeneutics of the Qur'an'. The document, they said, gave the impression of 'deliberate selectivity' with the aim of making Islam seem more open to dialogue and willing to understand than it could be on the basis of traditional exegesis of the Qur'an. It took 'considerable exegetical effort' to make the Qur'an, and in particular Sura 3:64, 'a scriptural basis for peaceful relations between Muslims and Christians', and those efforts had not been made here. Instead, the authors were using specific texts from the Qur'an and the Bible not to invite everyone to 'a common word' but rather to invite them to Islam. In this document Jesus in particular remained 'despite being clothed in the Bible, purely and simply the Jesus of the Qur'an!'. Another important point, it was said, was that the document did nothing to clarify the relationship between the Qur'an and Sharia – Islamic religious law. 'Put more bluntly: Not even

the most unambiguously formulated gestures of friend-
ship are worth the paper they are printed on if this does
not involve a redefinition of the Sharia-based relations
of Muslims to non-Muslims.' The argument in favour of
'freedom of religion' in Sura 3:64 of the Qur'an was said
to be based on a down-played exegesis![95]

The stance of the International Christian Network was
even clearer. This is, in essence, an association of Protestant fundamentalists. They too are unable to see a true
offer of dialogue in 'A Common Word', judging it instead
to be 'a call to unbelievers to convert to Islam and to sub-
jugate themselves'. Peace? 'Only by subjecting oneself to
Islam'. Bible quotations? Appropriated by Muslims! Vision
of love? Completely different from the Christian vision.
Islamic love was 'in the final analysis, self-love'! Freedom
of religion? Only the 'freedom to be able to practise Islam
without restrictions'. 'A fair society?' Only 'an Islamic
society'! The conclusion of the ICN's analysis:

'A Common Word' proves, after close analysis, to be
an injunction to give up Christ as the centre of their
faith and to limit the latter to the Islamic conception
of love of God = Allah and love of one's neighbour.
However, 'love of God' means something very
different in Islam than it does in the Bible. It means
subjugating oneself to the Islamic god and accepting
the Qur'an along with the introduction of Sharia law
as state law. There is no way that we Christians can get

involved with such an imposition without denying our Lord and Saviour.[96]

How do we react to this document and the criticisms of it? I cannot possibly engage in a long discussion on individual points here, however exciting that might be. I would, however, like to set out my general position, beginning with some positive conclusions:

(1) Countless times at events in recent years I have heard people remark regarding the possibility of inter-religious dialogue that 'the' Muslims do not want a dialogue. The only people who wanted a dialogue were a few starry-eyed liberal Christian theologians indulging in wishful thinking based on a harmless vision of Islam. The Document of the 138 disproves such claims. It responds to a challenge that many Christians interested in dialogue have been raising for years with their Muslim partners: Go on the offensive! Make it clear that interreligious dialogue can be a genuine concern for Muslims too. Show the public that Islam has the foundations on which to construct a dialogue.

(2) Focusing on the two Commandments about love satisfyingly subverts all the clichés about Islam that have taken root in public perception over recent years. These clichés present Islam as standing for aggressive fundamentalism, violence, the repression of freedom and the denial of human rights, especially with regard to women. It is certainly true that the public image of Islam in Europe is

not exactly dominated by the two Commandments about love. The signatories of the 'Common Word' letter strike a counterpoint to this, concluding: 'As Muslims, we say to Christians that we are not against them and that Islam is not against them.'

Critical questions

Yet there is certainly room for critical questions about the document, and I shall make a few important points.

1. The document invites Christians to enter into a dialogue, yet it ignores potential Jewish partners, even though the document refers explicitly at certain points to the Old Testament, the Jewish liturgy, Judaism and the Jews. The signatories know that the two Commandments about love were not 'invented' by Christians, but have their origins in the Old Testament and Jewish tradition. This unites Jews, Christians and Muslims. So why not involve Jewish partners? Why focus on an exclusive relationship between Christians and Muslims? Is this perhaps based on a latent or manifest superiority complex, a feeling that only Christianity and Islam are truly global religions, that the smaller faiths can be ignored? Or is it for political reasons, because a comment about Judaism is considered politically too sensitive?

The ecumenical objectives of this document would have more credibility if the dialogue were expanded to a trialogue!

2. There is an impressive focus in the choice of quotations from the Qur'an on love of God and love for one's neighbour, but not a word about other passages of the Qur'an that show glimpses of aggression towards Christians and 'infidels'. In particular, there is no mention of the relationship between the Qur'an and Sharia law. Naturally, one is not required to list every detail of what is a complex problem, but it would have been helpful to include a word of self-criticism about those in Muslim ranks who derive divisive ideas about unbelievers from the Qur'an – at the very least, a rule of interpretation about how the centre should deal with such passages in the future. Scholars of Islam are on firm ground when they criticise the document for having 'no coherent, viable hermeneutics of the Qur'an'.

3. The set of issues around 'freedom of religion' calls for special examination. There is legitimate doubt about whether Sura 2:256 and the commandment to love one's neighbour really do engender freedom of religion in the modern sense of the term. The modern understanding of religious freedom denotes three kinds of freedom: freedom *for* religion (being free to practise a religion),

freedom *of* religion (being free to change religion) and freedom *from* religion (being free to have no religion). The letter's authors have been challenged to show whether not just the first kind (the freedom to practise and propagate Islam) but also the other two kinds of freedom are compatible with the provisions of the Qur'an and the Sunna.

4. Does the document really respect the authority of the Christian Holy Scripture? We addressed this tricky subject in the second chapter of this book. The document appears to take a different course here. In any case, the Catholic scholar of Islam and Jesuit Christian Troll, a respected contributor to Christian-Muslim dialogue, noted: 'It is in itself a highly significant fact that this document includes a number of Biblical passages and comments positively on them. Does this indicate something of a break with Islamic doctrine, according to which the holy scriptures of the Jews and Christians (as they exist in their present form) are regarded as "corrupted" either by falsification of the text or by distortion of the meaning of the text (*tahrif al-nass; tahrif al-ma'na*)? As a consequence of this view, the great majority of Muslims have hitherto regarded the text of the Bible (in its present form) as unreliable, have generally taken little interest in its contents (except, in some cases, for polemical purposes) and have not recognised it as a

shared basis for dialogue. For example, the Book
of Psalms is not read by Muslims, either in public
liturgy or in private devotion, despite the fact that
the Qur'an repeatedly speaks of the Psalms which
were given by God to David (cf. Suras 4:163;
17:55). So one naturally asks whether the authors
of this document are seeking to understand the
biblical texts which they have cited in their own
authentically biblical context, which includes
both the immediate context of any particular text
and also the wider context of the whole Bible.
Or could it be that these biblical texts are only
accepted and quoted by the Muslim scholars in
so far as they correspond with the message of the
Qur'an?'[97]

Consensus about Jesus?

The document invites Christians to share a 'common
word' in the sense of Sura 3:64. This suggests a willing-
ness to engage in a conversation and an openness to dialogue. Admittedly, we did establish that the wording of
Sura 3:59–64 offers only a minimal consensus, but that
is already a decent start. We can answer for a number
of points of consensus when it comes to conceptions of
Jesus and God.

Regarding a consensus about God:

- Christians too wish to serve only the one and only true God in their faith and their lives. Their monotheism is not undermined by belief in Christ and the Son of God.
- Christians too understand their belief in Jesus of Nazareth as Christ and the Son of God not as an addition or 'association' (as if there were suddenly two Gods) but rather as a deepening of their understanding of God. God, the supreme 'Creator', is also the loving, conciliating 'Father' – an association that is based on the pronouncements of the historical Jesus himself (Matt. 6:9–15; Mark 11:25; Luke 11:2–4).
- Christians too radically reject any 'idolisation' of other things (people, powers, ideologies) in the name of the one and only true God.

As far as the conception of Jesus is concerned, an initial consensus could be established on the following basis. The message in Sura 3:59 ('In God's eyes Jesus is just like Adam: He created him from dust, said to him, "Be", and he was') can be fully assimilated by Christians too. We saw in our analysis of Luke 1:35 and Sura 21:91, in combination with the statement about the first man in Sura 15:28 ('Your Lord said to the angels, "I will create a mortal out of dried clay, formed from dark mud. When I have fashioned him and breathed My spirit into him, bow down before him"'), that there does not need to be any disagreement between Christians and Muslims on this point. According to the genealogy in Luke, as we heard, Jesus is a son of Adam, who in turn was created by God (Luke 3:38).

Christians and Muslims can at least approve of the following statement on the basis of their Holy Books (notwithstanding further dogmatic interpretations within Christianity):

Jesus is neither a man like other men nor 'God' (the father) nor a semi-divine being (in the mythological sense). Jesus' origin is in God himself, and thus he is only comparable to the very first creature, Adam. Just as God created Adam without presuppositions, so he created Jesus also. Just as Adam came to life without human participation, so Jesus was born without any male intervention by the creative power of God's word. Jesus' existence as God's messenger is the direct and immediate consequence of God's creative will.

Admittedly, this consensus is not sufficient for Christians. The criterion for the word to be 'common' cannot be defined by Muslims alone, since Sura 3:59–64 does not address the specific Christian belief that Jesus is the only son of God. We can therefore concur with Claus Schedl's analysis of this message in the Qur'an: 'These three contractual clauses are a theological document, but also a political and diplomatic one. Muhammad imposes quite a lot on his contractual partners. He demands nothing less than that they abandon their belief in the "son of God" and the veneration of the saints, because these constitute "associating" other beings to the "one God" as accessory gods. This was not at all the case from a Christian point of view, though, as they also believed in monotheism and did not interpret "associating" in the same way as Muhammad. There was therefore no theological settlement.'[98]

Thus, there can be no question of common ground between Christians and Muslims if we stick to the framework of Sura 3:59–64. Christians would have to disregard or even deny the core of their faith – Jesus as the son of God. The authors cannot establish 'common ground' simply by quoting Jesus' words in the Gospel According to Mark, for their document does even this with a modicum of self-interest. Muslims quote Mark's Gospel because it confirms their conception of God. Other 'Christological' clarifications of the Christian conception of God are omitted. Yet for Christians, 'Christology' can only be explored by the New Testament's standards, not the Qur'an's. Are Muslims prepared to pursue a conception of Jesus as the son of God that is not excluded by a verdict of 'idolisation'?

3. Christians and Islam's Holy Night

Whether the Document of the 138 has a future will depend, firstly, on whether Christians take the invitation seriously and the signatories of the letter at their word. Secondly, though, it will depend on whether it can prompt a self-critical discussion within the Muslim world. Just as important as the *inter-religious* dialogue is the *intra-religious* dialogue against the totalitarian-minded Islamists within. In the spirit of this document, however, both sides could begin to speak more self-critically than they have until now – about principles for interpreting the Qur'an, about relations between Muslims and non-Muslims, about relations between men and women, religion and politics, monotheism and Christology. That's a lot to get through. This invitation is an unprecedented signal that these issues can and must be tackled, and one that many Christians have long awaited.

Common tasks for the future

However Christians might assess this, they should at least agree with their Muslim partners about the starting point for this document: an analysis of the dramatic global context. The following passage in the document ought to be uncontroversial:

> Finding common ground between Muslims and Christians is not simply a matter for polite ecumenical dialogue between selected religious leaders. Christianity and Islam are the largest and second largest religions in the world and in history. Christians and Muslims reportedly make up over a third and

over a fifth of humanity respectively. Together they make up more than 55% of the world's population, making the relationship between these two religious communities the most important factor in contributing to meaningful peace around the world. If Muslims and Christians are not at peace, the world cannot be at peace. With the terrible weaponry of the modern world; with Muslims and Christians intertwined everywhere as never before, no side can unilaterally win a conflict between more than half of the world's inhabitants. Thus our common future is at stake. The very survival of the world itself is perhaps at stake.

And to those who nevertheless relish conflict and destruction for their own sake or reckon that ultimately they stand to gain through them, we say that our very eternal souls are all also at stake if we fail to sincerely make every effort to make peace and come together in harmony. God says in the Holy Qur'an: *Lo! God enjoineth justice and kindness, and giving to kinsfolk, and forbiddeth lewdness and abomination and wickedness. He exhorteth you in order that ye may take heed* (Al Nahl, 16:90). Jesus Christ said: *Blessed are the peacemakers* ....(Matthew 5:9), and also: *For what profit is it to a man if he gains the whole world and loses his soul?* (Matthew 16:26).

So let our differences not cause hatred and strife between us. Let us vie with each other only in righteousness and good works. Let us respect each other, be fair, just and kind to another and live in sincere peace, harmony and mutual goodwill.

In the prologue to this book, I reported that Muslims are already willing and able to present their best wishes to Christians on the feast of the Nativity. Muslims are already invited in many German cities to various Christmas festivities, both in church and outside. As we have established, the 'Holy Night', on which Christians commemorate the coming of Jesus Christ in special fashion, holds great significance for Muslims too.

Islam has its own Holy Night. Christians should not forget this, and they should pay their respects and present their good wishes to Muslims accordingly. Indeed, comparing these two Holy Nights could give rise to a profound discussion about the sign God gives to Christians and Muslims, and the extent to which this sign commits them to peace, bearing in mind that both the Qur'an and the New Testament call Jesus a sign of God's mercy and peace. In commemorating the birth of Jesus, Christians and Muslims could become benefactors and peacemakers for each other.

The Night of Decree

Conversely, Christians could also remind Muslims that the night of the revelation of the Qur'an is not only a 'Night of Decree' (*Laylat al-Qadr* in Arabic); it is also a night of commitment to peace, on which it is incumbent upon Muslims to love both God and their fellow man. The words of the Catholic theologian and commentator Eugen Drewermann are particularly apt in this regard: 'If we wanted to explain Christianity's Christmas message, for example, to a Muslim, we should not tell him first about the "virgin birth" of Jesus, which is related in the Qur'an, although not as the birth of a son of God. We should remind him of the blessed night of al-Qadr, when the angel Gabriel came down from the seventh heaven and revealed the suras to Muhammad – the Night of Power and Destiny, which brings "peace and salvation … until the flowering of the dawn". The important thing is to perceive and believe in something shining above us in the darkness, showing us the way. If we follow it we will find the "babe" that is born "immaculately" inside us on the spot where the "star" stops.'[99]

Exchanging messages of peace

It is true that Muslims commemorate the revelation of the Qur'an on their Holy Night. In the same way Jews mark the night of exodus as a time when the divine comes especially close, just as Christians mark their Holy Night at Christmas and at Easter, Muslims celebrate their special night in the month of Ramadan as the night when the divine revealed itself, according to Sura 97:

We sent it [the Qur'an] down on the Night of Glory.
What will explain to you what that Night of Glory is?
The Night of Glory is better than a thousand months;
on that night the angels and the Spirit descend again
and again with their Lord's permission on every task;
[there is] peace that night until the break of dawn.

(Sura 97:1–5)

The Holy Night of Islam is a time of special receptiveness among men for the coming of the divine, a time in which the heavens again become permeable to the earth, but equally a time of commitment to peace. Christians should take advantage of this night to exchange peaceful wishes with Muslims in the same way that Muslims have started to offer wishes of peace to Christians on the Holy Night of Jesus' birth. This is more than a gesture one makes to others; it is also an expression of one's commitment to live in peace. What did the Document of the 138 say again? 'If Muslims and Christians are not at peace, the world cannot be at peace.'

The 'Mary' Sura and the Example of Ethiopia

Some moments in life stay with you for ever. Some unexpected encounters leave a lasting impression. Around ten years ago I received a postcard from a certain Dr Asfa-Wossen Asserate in Frankfurt, asking me, in very elaborate calligraphic handwriting, if we might meet and talk. Soon afterwards, he is sitting opposite me in my study at the university, and I listen raptly to what my visitor has to say. This prince from Ethiopia's imperial family has been living in Germany for decades and studied Law in Tübingen.

Why does he want to speak to me? He has read my book about Abraham, in which I analysed his importance as a figure for Jews, Christians and Muslims, and developed the concept of 'Abrahamic ecumenism'. This theme is playing on his mind. I learn something that I didn't know until now: Ethiopia isn't only – as Western clichés would have it – a Christian country; many religions are represented on its territory. Just over 50% of Ethiopia's fifty million inhabitants are indeed members of the Ethiopian Orthodox Church, but 30–40% of the population are Sunni Muslims.

This is news to me. I know of Ethiopia's great Christian tradition stretching back to biblical times. I am also aware of the unimaginable fact that troops from Catholic Italy invaded Ethiopia in 1935 and occupied the country until 1941. Equally imprinted on my memory is 1960, a year that saw Ethiopia's first coup, which Emperor Haile Selassie was able to put down. Nor have I forgotten that the emperor was ignominiously overthrown by the military in September 1974. Lastly, I remember 'Bloody Saturday' in November 1974, when terror and death swept through Ethiopia. Some 60 people – the country's entire political elite including Prince Asserate's father – were murdered and buried in a mass grave in the grounds of Akaki prison in Addis Ababa. The emperor died a year later. The circumstances of his death remain unclear to this day, but there are further details in his biography, *King of Kings. The Triumph and the Tragedy of Emperor Haile Selassie of Ethiopia*, by Prince Asserate, the emperor's great-nephew.[100]

I am also aware of Islam's influence in North and Central Africa, of course, but I did not know that Ethiopia is effectively a country divided between two religions, and that conflicts have intermittently erupted between Christians and Muslims throughout its history, with renewed tensions today. Prince Asserate is worried that the violent upheavals in the Islamic world might exacerbate these tensions in the future. Ethiopia has not been unscathed by totalitarian Islam. Events on the other side of the Red Sea – from Syria, Palestine and Israel in the north to Yemen in the south – have always had an impact on the situation in Ethiopia.

But how can dialogue be set in motion? Do the foundations for a dialogue between Christians and Muslims exist? These were clearly the concerns that led Prince Asserate to pick up my book on Abraham and wish to discuss it with the author. Abraham may play a very different role in each tradition, but he can be a figure who unites Jews, Christians and Muslims at the level of their most deeply held beliefs. That is because Abraham perfectly illustrates what it comes down to when men meet their Maker: it is not human traditions and conventions that count, but radical trust in God as the creator, guardian and judge of the world. This trust stems from the conviction that all human beings, regardless of their religion, nationality and skin colour, are creatures of the same God and members of the same family of man.

I confess that that meeting with Prince Asserate made me see Ethiopian history through new eyes. I am more alive to news from that country than I used to be. I now have a face in my mind's eye that embodies Ethiopia. I see a man who is worried about the fate of his country, and his concern stems from his family history. At our first meeting I was pained to hear that it was the revolutionary turmoil afflicting his country in 1974 that had led to Prince Asserate's exile in Germany.

What a story! It is available as a memoir entitled *Ein*

Prinz aus dem Hause David (*A Prince of the House of David*, 2007), which I publicised at the prince's request in Tübingen on 19 January 2008. German readers will be surprised when the author states in the very first few pages, quite matter-of-factly, that he traces his ancestry back to King Solomon and the Queen of Sheba. Here before us is a man who can claim to be a 'Prince of the House of David'! We immediately envision the fascinating story of the Queen of Sheba's encounter with King Solomon as told in 1 Kings, chapter 10 and 2 Chronicles, chapter 9 of the Hebrew Bible. That is not all, though. The author can not only prove his descent from King David but also from the Prophet Muhammad. This is a deliberate signal to his countrymen, and I read: 'It is not least this part of my genealogy that may be the reason why I have studied Islam very closely in recent years.' This also explains why Prince Asserate read from his book on 11 March 2007 in Frankfurt's Icon Museum and also quoted from mine, *Vom Streit zum Weltstreit der Religionen. Lessing und die Herausforderung des Islam* (*From Disputes to Competition between the Religions. Lessing and the Challenge of Islam*).

After meeting Prince Asserate, I interpret Ethiopian history more attentively and with a newfound sensibility. I suddenly recall a highly symbolic scene, dating from the early days of Islam, which illustrates the relationship between Christians and Muslims. It takes place in Ethiopia at the beginning of the seventh century and was recorded by the Prophet Muhammad's first biographer, Ibn Ishaq, whom we discussed in the second chapter of this book. As we know, there is little or no historical basis for many of the events it reports, yet they often carry great symbolic meaning, particularly for a country like Ethiopia, which played an early and fundamental role in shaping relations between Christians and Muslims.

The seventh-century biographer describes an expedition by members of the original Muslim community to the court of the Negus (King) of Ethiopia, since their oppression by the Meccan establishment had become unbearable.[101] It is the year 615. The Meccans, furious at their fellow tribesmen's insubordination, send two envoys to Ethiopia, 'armed' with gifts. They demand that the 'fugitives' be handed over, if possible before the ruler has had an opportunity to talk to them. The Negus, however, shows his respect for the principle of hospitality. He would like to hear for himself the crime of which the emigrants stand accused. He summons bishops, who unroll their holy scriptures before him, and questions the Muslims about their new religion. When they refer to the teachings of their Prophet, the Negus asks to hear a sample passage. In response, one of the Muslims recites an excerpt from the 'Mary' sura, Sura 19, the sura of the annunciation and birth of Jesus, which this book has analysed in depth.

How did the Negus react? Ibn Ishaq's account records his response thus: 'The Negus wept until his beard became wet. His bishops also wept upon hearing what was recited to them until the scriptures became soaked.' The Christian authorities in Ethiopia were evidently deeply moved by the account of the annunciation to Mary and the birth of Jesus in Sura 19. The Meccan envoys' demands were therefore rejected: 'This and what Jesus taught must come from the same niche of light! By God, I shall not give them up to you and I shall not betray them!'

Yet the Meccans refused to let the matter lie. One of them appeared before the Negus again. The converts claimed 'terrible things about Jesus', he said. They considered the Son of Mary 'merely a man'! Once more the Ethiopian ruler summons the Muslims. Acutely aware of the stakes, they stick to what was 'taught' to their Prophet. They tell the Negus, 'We speak about him [Jesus] as we have been taught by our Prophet, namely that he is God's Servant, His Prophet, His Spirit and His Word, which He cast to the Virgin Mary.'

Once more, the Negus's reaction is unexpected. He picks up a stick from the ground and explains, 'By God, Jesus, son of Mary, does not exceed what you have just said by the length of this stick.' This time a murmur runs through the room. There is grumbling from the rows of generals surrounding the throne. They are obviously concerned about the orthodoxy of this pronouncement. The Ethiopian ruler repeats his opinion in even stronger terms. 'Though you snort, by God!' he says, and turning to the Muslims: 'Go, for you are safe in my country.' Then he repeated three times the words, 'He who curses you will be fined. Not for a mountain of gold would I allow a man of you to be hurt. Give them back their presents for I have no use for them. God took no bribe from me when He gave me back my kingdom; that I should take a bribe for it, and God did not do what men wanted against me, so why should I do what they want against Him.'[102]

What an incredible event played out on Ethiopian soil! The events are obviously stylised and recalled from a perspective that has Muslim interests in mind. Nonetheless, do they not reveal a great deal of wisdom about how Christians can get on with Muslims? The Ethiopian Christian king clearly adopts an intermediate position between obstinate Christian orthodoxy (the grumbling generals) and fanatical unbelief (the delegation from Mecca). This intermediate position combines tolerance with decisiveness, for this Christian king embodies a form of belief that accepts that it is impossible to measure people of another faith by the yardstick of one's own orthodoxy – or beat them with it.

This means that if non-Christians such as these Muslims state their belief in Jesus in terms describing him as 'God's Servant, His Prophet, His Spirit and His Word which He cast in the Virgin Mary', then that is sufficient for this Christian king. It is sufficient for him to take them in as guests in his land and protect them. He requires no more of them. He does not put them under pressure, judge them or demand the impossible. Christians will push Christology further; they will say more about Jesus, Christ and the Son of God, and express their faith in other ways. It is already significant for Muslims to be able to say that this special Messenger springs from God, speaks and acts with the power of God's spirit and is therefore an outstanding 'sign' of God for the whole world and for all men – a sign of God's 'mercy' (Sura 19:21); a messenger of God who can say of himself that God will bless him wherever he lives (Sura 19:31): 'Peace was on me the day I was born, and will be on me the day I die and the day I am raised to life again' (Sura 19:33).

In the early days of both Christianity and Islam, a meeting took place on Ethiopian soil that, regardless of its historical veracity, has lost none of its charm and truth today. The Muslim tradition commemorates Ethiopia as a land in which a scene of universal significance took place – a scene whose message is still to be heard by many Christians and Muslims. Ethiopia could become a country of exemplary communication, mutual respect and peaceful coexistence between Christians and Muslims. It would be tragic were the opposite to occur.

References

THE BIBLE
Unless stated otherwise, Biblical texts are quoted from the New King James Version.

THE QUR'AN
Texts from the Qur'an are quoted from M. A. S. Abdel Haleem's translation, Oxford 2008, and occasionally from Alan Jones's translation, Cambridge 2007.

EQ
Jane Dammen McAucliffe (ed.), *Encyclopaedia of the Qur'an*, Vols I-IV, Leiden – Boston – Cologne 2001–04.

KKK
Der Koran. Arabisch-Deutsch. Translation and scholarly commentary by Adel Theodor Khoury, Vols. I-IX, Gütersloh 1990–2001.

NKTS
Angelika Neuwirth, *Der Koran als Text der Spätantike. Ein europäischer Zugang*, Frankfurt am Main 2010.

NKK
Angelika Neuwirth, *Der Koran. Bd. I: Frühmekkanische Suren. Prophetische Prophetie*, Frankfurt am Main 2011.

Bibliography

Primary literature

I. Editions and general reference

1. Post-Biblical texts:
J.K. Elliott, *The Apocryphal New Testament. A Collection of Apocryphal Christian Literature in an English Translation*, Oxford 2005. Based on: (M.R. James, *The Apocryphal New Testament - Translation and Notes*, Oxford 1924.

W. Schneemelcher (ed.), *New Testament Apocrypha*. English translation edited by R. McL. Wilson. Vol I (*Gospels and Related Writings*), Louisville – London, revised edition 1991.

2. Qur'anic and post-Qur'anic texts:
The Qur'an. Translated by M. A. S. Abdel Haleem, Oxford 2004.
The Qur'an. Translated by Alan Jones, Cambridge 2007.
The Life of Muhammad. A Translation of Ishaq's Sirat Rasol Allah with Introduction and Notes by Alfred Guillaume, Oxford 1955.

3. More recent general reference works:
H. Küng, *Christianity: Essence, History, Future*, London – New York 1995.

H. Küng, *Islam: Past, Present and Future*, London 2007.

K-J. Kuschel, *Juden – Christen – Muslime: Herkunft und Zukunft* (*Jews – Christians – Muslims. Origins and Future* – untranslated), Düsseldorf 2007.

4. More recent literature on the impact of the Prophet:

H. Jansen, *Muhammad: The Mecca and Medina Stories*, Amherst, NY 2012.

T. Nagel, *Mohammed. Leben und Legende* (*Muhammad: Life and Legend*), Munich 2008.

A. Schimmel, *And Muhammad is His Messenger: The Veneration of the Prophet in Islamic Piety*, Chapel Hill 1985.

Secondary literature:

1. Recent commentaries:

(1) On Matthew's Gospel:

H. Frankemölle, *Matthäus-Kommentar* (*Commentary on Matthew's Gospel*) Vol. I, Düsseldorf 1994.

U. Luz, *Das Evangelium nach Matthäus*. 1. Teilband: Matthäus 1–7 (*The Gospel According to Matthew. I. Vol: Matthew*), Düsseldorf – Zurich – Neukirchen-Vluyn, 5th edition 2002.

(2) On Luke's Gospel:

F. Bovon, *Das Evangelium nach Lukas*, 1. Teilband: Lk 1,1–9,50 (*The Gospel According to Luke*), Zurich – Neukirchen-Vluyn 1989.

2. On New Testament account of the birth of Jesus:

R.E. Brown, *The Birth of the Messiah. A Commentary on the Infancy Narratives in the Gospels of Matthew and Luke*, New York/London 1993.

E. Drewermann, *Licht des Friedens. Meditationen zum Advent und zur Weihnacht* (*Light of Peace. Meditations about Advent and Christmas*), Düsseldorf 2004.

W. Jens (ed.), *Es begibt sich aber zu der Zeit. Texte zur Weihnachtsgeschichte* (*It Happens At This Time. Texts on the History of Christmas*), Stuttgart 1988.

R. Pesch, *Das Weihnachtsevangelium* (*The Christmas Gospel*)
Freiburg/Br. 2007.

P. Stuhlmacher, *Die Geburt des Immanuel. Die
Weihnachtsgeschichten aus dem Lukas und Matthäus-Evangelium*
(*The Birth of Immanuel. The Christmas Stories from Luke's and
Matthew's Gospels*), Göttingen 2005.

G. Vermes, *The Nativity: History and Legend*, New York 2007.

3. On the story of Jesus' birth in the Qur'an:

(1) From a Christian perspective:

M. Bauschke, *Der Sohn Marias. Jesus im Koran* (*The Son of Mary.
Jesus in the Qur'an*), Darmstadt 2013.

Pulsfort E. & Hagemann L., Maria, *die Mutter Jesu, in Bibel und
Koran* (*Mary, Mother of Jesus, in the Bible and the Qur'an* –
untranslated), Würzburg – Altenberge 1992.

O. Leirvik, *Images of Jesus Christ in Islam*, Uppsala 1999, Ch. II/1:
Christ in the Qur'an.

K-J. Kuschel, *Juden – Christen – Muslime: Herkunft und Zukunft*
(*Jews – Christians – Muslims. Origins and Future* – untranslated),
Düsseldorf 2007, Part V: 'Maria und Jesus oder: Zeichen Gottes
für alle Welt'.

S. A. Mourad, 'From Hellenism to Christianity and Islam: The Origin
of the Palm Tree Story Concerning Mary and Jesus in the Gospel
of Pseudo-Matthew and the Qur'an', in: *Oriens Christianus* 86
(2002), pp. 206–16.

A. Neuwirth, 'Imagining Mary, Disputing Jesus: Reading Surat
Maryam (Q 19) and Related Meccan Texts in the Context
of the Qur'anic Communication Process / Mary and Jesus:
Counterbalancing the Biblical Patriarchs. A Re-Reading of
Surat Maryam (Q 19) in Surat Al 'Imran (Q 3)', in: A. Neuwirth,
*Scripture, Poetry and the Making of a Community. Reading the
Qur'an as a Literary Text,* Oxford 2014, pp. 328–58 /pp. 359–84.

H. Räisänen, 'The Portrait of Jesus in the Qur'an: Reflections of a Biblical Scholar', in: *Muslim World* 70 (1980), pp. 122–33.

C. Schedl, *Muhammad und Jesus. Die christologisch relevanten Texte des Korans* (*Muhammad and Jesus: Christologically Relevant Texts in the Qur'an*), Vienna – Freiburg/Br. – Basel 1978, pp 175–206 (Sura 19), pp. 374–445 (Sura 3).

K. v. Stosch / M. Khorchide (ed.), *Streit um Jesus. Muslimische und christliche Annäherungen* (*Disputing Jesus. Muslim and Christian Rapprochement* – untranslated*)*, Paderborn 2016.

(2) From a Muslim perspective:

N. Akin, *Untersuchungen zur Rezeption des Bildes von Maria und Jesus in den frühislamischen Geschichtsüberlieferungen* (*Studies of the Reception of the Image of Mary and Jesus in Early Islamic Historical Accounts*), Ladenburg 2002.

M. Andaç, *Einladung zum Islam. Ein Vergleich zwischen Bibel und Koran aus der Sicht eines Moslems* (*An Invitation to Islam. Comparing the Bible and the Qur'an from a Muslim Perspective*), Berlin 2000.

M. Bazargan, *Und Jesus ist ein Prophet. Der Koran und die Christen* (*And Jesus is His Prophet. The Qur'an and Christians*). Translated from Persian into German by Markus Gerhold, edited and introduced by Navid Kermani, Munich 2006, p. 41.

H.I. Çinar, *Maria und Jesus im Islam. Darstellung anhand des Korans und der islamischen kanonischen Tradition unter Berücksichtigung der islamischen Exegeten* (*Mary and Jesus in Islam*), Wiesbaden 2007.

A. Ginaidi, *Jesus Christ and Mary from a Qur'anic-Islamic Perspective: Fundamental Principles for Dialogue between Islam and Christianity*, Stuttgart 2005.

T. Khalidi, *The Muslim Jesus. Sayings and Stories in Islamic Literature*, Cambridge, Mass./London 2001.

A. Schimmel, *Jesus und Maria in der islamischen Mystik* (*Jesus and Mary in Islamic Mysticism*), Munich 1996.

4. On the Bible and the Qur'an:

A. Th. Khoury, *Der Koran, erschlossen und kommentiert* (*The Qur'an Explained and Commented*), Düsseldorf 2005, chapter on *Offenbarung und Propheten* (*Revelation and Prophets*), pp. 170–99.

K.-J. Kuschel, *Festmahl am Himmelstisch. Wie Mahlfeiern Juden, Christen und Muslime verbindet* (*A Feast at the Heavenly Table. How Ritual Suppers Bring Jews, Christians and Muslims Together* – untranslated), Stuttgart-Ostfildern 2013.

ibid. *Die Bibel im Koran. Grundlagen für das interreligiöse Gespräch* (*The Bible in the Qur'an. A Basis for Inter-religious Dialogue* – untranslated), Stuttgart – Ostfildern 2017.

R. Paret, *Mohammed und der Koran. Geschichte und Verkündigung des arabischen Propheten* (*Muhammad and the Qur'an. History and Promulgation of the Arab Prophet* – untranslated), Stuttgart 1957, 7th edition 1991.

Notes

1   http://www.vatican.va/roman_curia/pontifical_councils/
     interelg/documents/rc_pc_interelg_doc_20080430_rome-
     declaration_en.html

2   Quotations from the Qur'an are from M. A. S. Abdel Haleem's
     translation, Oxford 2008, and occasionally from Alan Jones's
     translation, Cambridge 2007.

3   SCM Press, New York 1995.

4   Patmos, Ostfildern, 2017.

5   This article was made available to me by Mr Şükrü Bulut (now
     in Cologne), who played a leading role in the establishment
     of the mosque and Islamic community in Ahlen. I am very
     grateful to Mr Bulut for providing me with this document and
     other material as well as for his commitment to promoting
     better understanding between Muslims and Christians in
     Germany.

6   The text of 'A Common Word' is available online at www.
     acommonword.com along with a compilation of the various
     responses to it.

7   More detail on this at www.duaatalislam.com

8   For more on the relationship between the Bible and
     the Qur'an, see Karl-Josef Kuschel, *Die Bibel im Koran.
     Grundlagen für das interreligiöse Gespräch,* Stuttgart-
     Ostfildern 2017.

9   This is a quotation from Walter Jens's introduction,
     as editor, to *Es begibt sich aber zu der Zeit. Texte zur
     Weihnachtsgeschichte,* Stuttgart 1988, p. 12.

10   More on this in Chapter 10 ('Infancy Gospels') in W.
        Schneemelcher (ed.), *New Testament Aprocrypha*. Vol. I
        (Gospels), Louisville – London 1991.

11   The passages that follow are quoted from the New King James
        Version of the Bible.

12   I quote the most comprehensive commentary available by U.
        Lutz, *Das Evangelium nach Matthäus*. 1.Teilband: Matthäus
        1–7, Düsseldorf – Zürich – Neukirchen-Vluyn, 5th edition
        2002, p. 126.

13   For an overview of the latest research see also: H. Förster,
        *Die Feier der Geburt Christi in der Alten Kirche. Beiträge
        zur Erforschung der Anfänge des Epiphanie- und des
        Weihnachtsfest* (*The Feast of the Birth of Jesus in the Ancient
        Church. Articles about the Origins of Epiphany and Christmas*),
        Tübingen 2000; ibid., *Die Anfänge von Weihnachten
        und Epiphanias* (*The Origins of Christmas and Epiphany –
        untranslated*), Tübingen 2007.

14   In two major publications the Vienna-based Coptologist and
        papyrus specialist Hans Förster contradicted the widespread
        belief that the Christian feast of Christmas had pagan roots
        because it was meant to replace the Roman Empire's Sol
        Invictus festival. This theory was subsequently rejected by the
        ancient historian Alexander Demandt. He accuses Förster of
        only mentioning the main ancient source for the Sol Invictus
        festival second-hand in two footnotes, thereby trivialising
        it. Demandt notes that the Sun God's birthday was 'a very
        popular and originally "religious" festival in broadly pagan late
        antiquity'. The 'link between Jesus' birthday and the solstice'
        was 'clearly underlined' by the Fathers of the Church. Förster
        acknowledged this, but nonetheless maintained that this
        was related to 'astronomical facts' but not to the Sol Invictus

festival. 'Who will buy that?' (*Süddeutsche Zeitung*, 24–26 December 2007).

15   P. Stuhlmacher, *Die Geburt des Immanuel. Die Weihnachtsgeschichten aus dem Lukas- und Matthäus-Evangelium*, Göttingen 2nd edition 2006, pp. 34–35.

16   H. Frankenmölle, *Matthäus-Kommentar* Vol. I, Düsseldorf 1994, 2nd edition 1999, pp. 152–53.

17   Translated from the German by Martin L. Seltz.

18   See W. Jens, *Die Evangelisten als Schriftsteller* (*The Evangelists as Authors*), in: ibid., *Republikanische Reden* (*Republican Speeches*), Munich 1976, pp. 30–40.

19   R. Pesch, *Das Weihnachtsevangelium* (*The Christmas Gospel. A new translation and edition*), Freiburg/Br. 2007, p. 79f.

20   *Die Bibel*. Erschlossen und kommentiert von H. Halbfas, Düsseldorf 2001, p. 421.

21   W. Jens, Introduction, p. 12 (see Note 6 above).

22   H. Küng, *On Being a Christian*. Translated by Edward Quinn. New York 1976. pp. 452–53.

23   Translated from the Swedish by Theophil Menzel, 1960.

24   English translation by the author, Chapel Hill 1985.

25   Mohammad Suliman al-Ashqer, *Your Way to Islam*. Raleigh 1995.

26   I. Kathir, *Stories of the Prophets*. Translated by Abd El Qader A. – Al Azeez H. Exclusive rights from: Dar Al-Ghad – Al-Gadeed, Egypt – Al-Mansoura.

27   Al-Sheikh Muhammad Ali Sabuni, *Prophethood and the Prophets*, translated by Mohammad Idris Esau, Saida/Lebanon undated.

28   Ibid., pp. 195–96.

29   Ibid., p. 212.

30   *The Life of Muhammad. A Translation of Ishaq's Sirat Rasol Allah*, with Introduction and Notes by Alfred Guillaume, Oxford 1955, p. 3.

31   T. Andræ, *Die Person Muhammads in Lehre und Glauben seiner Gemeinde*, Stockholm 1918, pp. 28–29.

32   T. Nagel, *Der Koran. Einführung – Texte – Erläuterungen (The Qur'an. Introduction – Texts – Explanations)*, Munich 1991, pp. 122–23.

33   A. Guillaume, op. cit. The following quotations are taken from the sections 'Of the Woman Who Offered Herself in Marriage to Abdullah', 'What Was Said to Amina When She Conceived the Apostle' and 'The Birth of the Apostle and His Suckling', pp. 68–73.

34   Quoted from *Der Koran, erschl. u. kommentiert* by A. Th. Khoury, Düsseldorf 2005, p. 36.

35   Translation quoted in *The Birth of the Prophet Muhammad. Devotional Piety in Sunni Islam* by M. Holmes Katz, Abingdon-on-Thames 2007, p. 33.

36   A. Guillaume, op. cit., p. 72.

37   M. Holmes Katz, op. cit., p. 33.

38   T. Andræ, op. cit.

39   H. Jansen, *Muhammad: The Mecca and Medina Stories*, Amherst, NY 2012. Translated by Brian Doyle, p. 33–34.

40   T. Khalidi, *The Muslim Jesus. Sayings and Stories in Islamic Literature*, Cambridge, Mass. – London 2001, p. 82.

41   Ibid., p. 120.

42   *Der Koran für Kinder und Erwachsene*, translated and explained by L. Kaddor & R. Müller, Munich 2008, p. 180.

43   Details about the presence of Christianity during the pre-Islamic era in: H. Küng, *Der Islam: Past, Present and Future*. Translated by John Bowden, Oxford 2007, pp. 32–44 & pp. 494–95.

On the subject of Christianity and Christians in the Qur'an: J. Wardenburg, 'Koranisches Religionsgespräch. Eine Skizze', in: *Studies in the History of Religions. Liber amicorum in Honour of C.J. Bleeker*, Leiden 1969, pp. 208–53; ibid., 'Towards a Periodisation of Earliest Islam According to its Relations with Other Religions', in: *The Qur'an: Style and Contents*, A. Rippin (ed.), Aldershot, VT 2001, pp. 93–115. J. Dammen McAucliffe, 'Christians in the Qur'an and Tafsir', in: *Muslim Perceptions of Other Religions. A Historical Survey*, J. Wardenburg (ed.), New York – Oxford 1999, pp. 105–21; E. Gräf, 'Zu den christlichen Einflüssen im Koran', in: *Al-Bahit. FS Joseph Henninger zum 70. Geburtstag*, St. Augustin 1976, pp. 111–44. S.H. Griffith, 'Art. Christians and Christianity', in: EQ I, pp. 307–15.
 On representations of Christian beliefs in classic Muslim commentary: N. Robinson, *Christ in Islam and Christianity. Representation of Jesus in the Qur'an and Classical Muslim Commentaries*, New York 1991; ibid., 'Christian and Muslim Perspectives on Jesus in the Qur'an', in: *Fundamentalism and Tolerance. An Agenda for Theology and Society*, A. Linzey & P. Wexler (eds.), London 1991, pp. 92–105; ibid. 'Jesus and Mary in the Qur'an: Some Neglected Affinities', in: *The Qur'an: Style and Contents*, A. Rippin (ed.), Aldershot, VT 2001, pp. 21–35.
On the further history of the influence of Christian belief in the Islamic world: L. Ridgeon (ed.), *Islamic Interpretations of Christianity*, Richmond, GB 2001.

44   K. v. Stosch & M. Khorchide (eds.) *Streit um Jesus*, Paderborn 2016, p. 17.

45   For details see A. Rippin, 'John the Baptist' in EQ 3, pp. 51–52.

46   KKK 4:25.

47   NKTS, p. 475.

48   NKTS, p. 472.

49   C. Schedl, *Mohammed und Jesus* (*Muhammad and Jesus*), Freiburg/B. 1978, p. 193.

50   For further details see H. Busse, *Islamische Erzählungen von Propheten und Gottesmännern*, Wiesbaden 2006, p. 483.

51   M. Bauschke, *Der Sohn Marias* (*The Son of Mary*), Bauschke 2013, p. 18.

52   W. Schneemelcher (ed.), *New Testament Apocrypha*, Translated by R. McL. Wilson. Vol. 1, 1991, pp. 421–38.

53   A. Neuwirth, *Imagining Mary, Disputing Jesus*, 2014, p. 339.

54   Schneemelcher, op. cit., *Protevangelium of James*, p. 426.

55   H. Busse, *Islamische Erzählungen von Propheten und Gottesmännern*, 2006, p. 485.

56   For suggested parallels with worship of Apollo at his temple on the island of Delos, see S.A. Mourad, *From Hellenism to Christianity and Islam*, 2002.

57   See W. Schneemelcher, ed. *New Testament Aprocrypha*, Vol. 1, 1991, pp. 462–5.

58   Ibid., p. 463.

59   See the Prologue in *Abraham – Father of the Faith for Three Religions*.

60   A. Neuwirth, 'Imagining Mary, Disputing Jesus' in Jokisch B. Rebstock U. and Conrad L. I. (eds.), *Fremde, Feinde und Kurioses: Innen- und Aussenansichten unseres muslimischen Nachbarn*, Berlin 2009, p. 413.

61   A. Neuwirth, 'Mary and Jesus: Counterbalancing the Biblical Patriarchs', in: *Parole de l'Orient* 30 (2005), p. 234.

62   For details see KKK, 4, pp. 79–81. R. Tottoli, in: EQ 2, p. 509.

63   'Protevangelium of James', in: R. F. Hock, *The Infancy Gospels of James and Thomas*, Santa Rosa, CA 1996.

64   A. Neuwirth, 'Mary and Jesus', p. 234.

65   Ibid.

66 A. Neuwirth, 'The House of Abraham and the House of Amran', in: *The Qur'an in Context*, Leiden – Boston 2010, p. 520.

67 Schneemelcher, op. cit., *Protevangelium of James*, p. 427.

68 For details see A. Schimmel, *Jesus und Maria in der islamischen Mystik*, Munich 1996; B. Freyer Stowasser, 'Mary', in: EQ 3, pp. 288–96.

69 L. Hagemann & E. Pulsfort, *Maria, die Mutter Jesu*, 1992, p. 97f.

70 F. Bovon, *Das Evangelium nach Lukas*, 1. Teilband: Lk 1:1–9:50, Zurich – Neukirchen-Vluyn 1989, pp. 131–32.

71 M. Andaç, *Einladung zum Islam. Ein Vergleich zwischen Bibel und Koran aus der Sicht eines Moslems* (*An Invitation to Islam. Comparing the Bible and the Qur'an from a Muslim Perspective*), Berlin 2000; N. Akin, *Untersuchungen zur Rezeption des Bildes von Maria und Jesus in den frühislamischen Geschichtsüberlieferungen* (*Studies of the Reception of the Image of Mary and Jesus in Early Islamic Historical Accounts*), Ladenburg 2002; A. Ginaidi, *Jesus Christ and Mary from a Qur'anic-Islamic Perspective: Fundamental Principles for Dialogue between Islam and Christianity*, Stuttgart 2005.

72 A. Schimmel, op. cit., p. 141.

73 Ibid.

74 Details in W. Vordtriede, 'Clemens Brentanos Anteil an der Kultstätte in Ephesus', in: *Deutsche Vierteljahrsschrift für Literaturwissenschaft und Geistesgeschichte* 34 (1960), pp. 384–401.

75 Details in D. Carrol, *Mary's House. The Extraordinary Story Behind the Discovery of the House Where the Virgin Mary Lived and Died*, London 2000.

76   A. Ihsan Yitik, 'Die Jungfrau Maria und ihr Haus bei Ephesus. Eine religionsvergleichende mariologische Untersuchung', in: *Journal of Religious Culture* 56 (2002), p. 4. Following this quotation the author reports on some of the impressive entries in the guestbook in the House of Mary in Ephesus. They express the fears, miseries, complaints and requests to Mary, written by ordinary people. The author's conclusion: 'It seems that for some visitors the Virgin Mary herself finds solutions to all kinds of problems, whereas for another section of visitors she is a kind of intermediary who presents their wishes to God. Those praying believe that wishes that take this path have an extremely good chance of being fulfilled, as Mary is a believer beloved of God to whom he can refuse nothing' (p. 6).

77   R. Kühn, *Bericht von einer Reise nach Selçuk* (*Account of a Journey to Selçuk*), June 2000. I have access to the manuscript.

78   Text available at: https://w2.vatican.va/content/benedict-xvi/en/homilies/2006/documents/hf_ben-xvi_hom_20061129_ephesus.html

79   L. Kaddor & R. Müller, op. cit., pp. 225–28.

80   Ibid., pp. 180–82

81   T. Khalidi, op. cit., pp. 180–82.

82   NKTS, pp. 472–73.

83   K. v. Stosch and M. Khorchide, op. cit., p. 51.

84   NKTS, p. 491.

85   NKTS, pp. 491–94.

86   NKTS, p. 492, p. 494.

87   *Und Jesus ist sein Prophet: Der Koran und die Christen*. German translation from the Persian by Markus Gerhold, Munich 2006, p. 42.

88   *The Apocryphal New Testament,* M.R. James – Translation and Notes, Oxford 1924.

89   K. v. Stosch and M. Khorchide, op. cit., p. 54.

90   More on this in K.-J. Kuschel, *Festmahl am Himmelstisch* (*A Feast at the Heavenly Table*), 2013, Ch. VI.

91   Ibid., p. 87.

92   Details in A. Th. Khoury, KK IV, pp. 123–29.

93   A. Th. Khoury, KK IV, p. 126. 'Der Text des Abkommens' ('The Text of the Agreement'), pp. 126–27. See also: A. Th. Khoury, *Muhammad. Der Prophet und seine Botschaft* (*The Prophet and His Message*), Freiburg/Br. 2008 (updated and expanded edition): 'Given the state of the legal and historical sources, which ascribe barely any, or much less, importance to the Ordal in this context, one may say that it cannot be taken as read that there is a direct link between the verses of the Qur'an quoted here and the events involving the delegation from Najran. Perhaps the many details were only given to provide an appropriate framework for the verses. From the point of view of theological and pious literature, the Ordal is important as a means of establishing the truth and confirming Muhammad's prophetic mission and the undeniable superiority of Islam over any other religion' (p. 132).

94   www.zenit.org/article-13926?/=german

95   This is summary of the main points of criticism presented by the Tübingen-based scholar of Islam L. Richter-Bernburg in *Ein 'Wort des Ausgleichs' für die monotheistischen Religionen? 138 muslimische Religionsgelehrte an die christlichen Kirchen*, published in a Festschrift for the Göttingen scholar of Islam Tilman Nagel. I have the manuscript, which the author kindly made available to me.

96   Internationale Konferenz bekennender Gemeinschaften/ International Christian Network (ed.), *Zum Brief von 138 muslimischen Gelehrten an die Christenheit. Erläuterungen und Hintergrundinformationen für christliche Leser* (*Response to the Letter signed by 138 Muslim scholars to Christians.*

Explanations and Background Information for Christian Readers).

97   http://www.acommonword.com/response-from-prof-dr-christian-troll-s-j/

98   C. Schedl, op. cit., pp. 441–42.

99   E. Drewermann, *Licht des Friedens. Meditationen zum Advent und zur Weihnacht* (*Light of Peace. Meditations about Advent and Christmas*), Düsseldorf 2004, p. 83.

100   Haus Publishing, London 2015.

101   A. Guillaume, op. cit.

102   Ibid. pp. 152–53